Swing the Hammer

Swing the Hammer

Use Money as a Tool

For Personal Happiness, Strong Marriage,
and Raising Terrific Kids

Brian Parker Sullivan

\// **Victoria Parker Books**
Vivere Aliis Servire

Copyright (c) 2023 Victoria Parker Books, Hartford Connecticut
All rights reserved. This book or parts thereof may not be reproduced in any form, stored in any retrieval system, or transmitted in any form by any means—electronic, mechanical, photocopy, recording, or otherwise—without prior written permission of the publisher, except as provided by United States of America copyright law. For permission requests, write to the publisher, at "Attention: Permissions Coordinator," at the address below.

Library of Congress Cataloging-in-Publication Data

ISBN: 979-8-9895369-2-4

Requests:	Victoria Parker Books, LLC
314 Farmington Avenue, Suite 100
Farmington, Connecticut 06032

To my father, who taught me consistency, allowed me to fail and learn, and showed me that happiness is not inherited.

Table of Contents

Acknowledgments..ix

The book in 3 pages...xi

Foreword..xv

Preface..xxi

Introduction..xxix

Don't Eat the Doughnut..1

Happiness Formula..11

Money Math..25

Buckets of Cash..39

OPA! Working Freedom..53

Risk of Life..63

Marriage and Money..77

Kids and Money..87

Connie and Glen Test..117

Acknowledgments

This book is an anthology of experiences I've had with many clients over the years. To those I've been able to talk with about this book, thank you for letting me share. For the families of those who have died, I wish they were here too. They were wonderfully important role models for me.

The grind of writing this book could not have been bearable without my business partner Iris. She has read every word, every rewrite, and countless pages that will never be read again. You've watched me evolve as a writer and slip into fanaticism over word counts. Thank you. (48)

Gratitude to my mentors who've guided, encouraged , and challenged me. Your support through phone calls, Zoom meetings, writing sessions, and emails has kept me on track. Jocko and the EF brigade, Shona and her band of local writers, and Scotty, the depth of your giving is stunning.

Special thanks to Rick Callahan and his team at Krative, LLC in New Haven, CT. They are masterminds in branding and marketing. His creative prowess brought my ideas to life through captivating visuals, websites, videos, and now, this book. Grateful for your invaluable expertise and dedication.

Finally, to my wife, Hilary, thank you. You reminded me to be tenacious, but helpful. Be loving but independent. Strong but tender. You are the fulcrum of my life.

Like most important things, this is

SIMPLE

Like most important things, this is not

EASY

75% of American adults experience monthly anxiety over **MONEY**

 The #1 disability in America is **DEPRESSION**

#1 cause of non-chemical depression is **FINANCIAL ANXIETY**

ACCOUNTS ARE NOT INVESTMENTS

· TIME ·

Your time is a field.
Neglect it and it will die.

Take action and you will reap years of benefits.

Investing is like **YARD WORK**, not a night at the **CASINO**

THESE ARE DIFFERENT!

 **FINANCIAL SECURITY**

FINANCIAL FREEDOM

 **FINANCIAL INDEPENDENCE**

Just because you have a hammer, it doesn't mean you're a carpenter.

Just because you have money, it doesn't mean you're happy.

Let us help you swing the hammer.

There are four ways to approach a **RISK**.

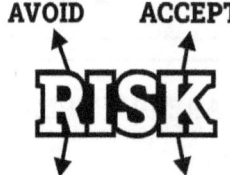

AVOID ACCEPT
REDUCE TRANSFER

TEACHING KIDS ABOUT
MONEY

- Purpose of Money
  Value Exchange
- Forms of Money
- Income Types
  Active, Passive, Portfolio
- Financial Fitness
  Good Habits

Money is a tool to achieve a

GOAL

Money is not a **GOAL**.   The **GOAL** is happiness.

ACHIEVEMENT

TOO MUCH    TOO LITTLE

LEADS TO HUBRIS   LEADS TO YIELDING

CONTENTMENT

TOO MUCH   TOO LITTLE

LEADS TO BOREDOM   LEADS TO ANXIETY

CONNECTION

TOO MANY    TOO LITTLE

BECOMES SUPERFICIAL   LEADS TO LONELINESS

OPA
Organize **P**rioritize **A**chieve

```
H   O   G   G
A   W   E   I
V   E   T   V
E           E
```

**WE DON'T SPEND MONEY.
WE CHOOSE WHO TO GIVE IT TO.**

Goals are good...

 Waypoints are **BETTER**

Completing a 60% plan is better than waiting for a 100% plan.

Confirmed Motivated Alignment:

CLARITY OF INTENT 👁
+
 CHOSEN INTENSITY

MONEY & MARRIAGE

✅ Life gets a vote. Blame is pointless.

EMBARRASSMENT to SHAME to DEFENSIVENESS to HIDING to FINANCIAL INFIDELITY.

Money is taboo, so when we need to talk about it, we **STINK**.

- Your relationship with **MONEY**
- Your relationship with your **SPOUSE**
- Your marriage relationship with **MONEY**

4 RULES OF FINANCIAL MARRIAGE

- Teamwork
- OPA
- Simple Plans
- Trust

PURPOSE OF MONEY

MONEY FACILITATES VALUE EXCHANGE

FAVOR
Kindness without specific return

BARTER
Direct swapping of goods and services

PAYMENT
Transfer of money for goods and services

CREDIT
Lending with future repayment expectation

Foreword

Dr. William A. Petit, Jr.

Stress and anxiety afflict many of us, particularly amidst the ongoing pandemic crisis. We face increased isolation, depression, thoughts of suicide, and concerns about the climate, all of which contribute to heightened stress levels. When we add the weight of our financial future into the equation, it creates a potential for poor decision-making. Many individuals need a reset or a different approach, one that addresses not only our emotional well-being and needs but also our financial challenges. We need a perspective that goes beyond mere number-crunching and delves into the core of our relationships with ourselves, our families, and our money. "Swing the Hammer" is not your typical financial planning manual; it is a journey into the heart and soul of economic well-being, a journey that has the potential to profoundly impact your overall health.

My friend, Brian Sullivan, has authored a groundbreaking perspective. Brian is more than just an author; he is a caring husband, father, son, mentor, and a sage in financial wisdom. He is a leader who understands the significance of hands-on personal assistance during times of financial distress. Brian holds two master's degrees and a certificate in financial planning from the College of Financial Planning. He is both an educator and a practitioner. Having known Brian for over 15 years, I have witnessed his unwavering commitment to alleviating financial anxieties in others. He doesn't merely offer advice; he engages in the art of healing through financial enlightenment. In "Swing the Hammer," he generously shares his invaluable insights and wisdom with all of us.

The central message of this book is deceptively simple but has the potential to profoundly transform your relationship with money, which, for all of us at varying levels, is inherently linked to our overall well-being. Brian uncovers a startling fact: a comprehensive seven-year study by the American Psychiatric Association has identified depression as the leading disability in America, with financial anxiety ranking as the top non-chemical cause. An astonishing 75% of adults in America grapple with significant economic pressure monthly. If this resonates with you, please understand that you are not alone, and there is hope.

"Swing the Hammer" provides a framework for achieving financial wellness and emotional healing. It begins by challenging our conventional understanding of money, compelling us to reevaluate its central role in our lives. Are we using money to attain happiness, contentment, and meaningful relationships, or has it primarily become a source of stress, anxiety, and emotional turmoil?

Brian adeptly guides us through the transformative process of viewing money as a tool for achieving success, contentment, and building connections. He offers practical advice and innovative approaches, such as the ACC Happiness Formula, The 4 Rules of Financial Marriage, and strategies for acquiring and maintaining motivation. These methods make financial planning more approachable and less intimidating, even for complex concepts like balance sheets, cash flow statements, and budgeting. If you've ever found these financial tasks overwhelming, rest assured—Brian introduces the HOGG method, a refreshing and user-friendly alternative.

As we all know, marriage often marks a significant turning point in our financial well-being. Brian offers guidance on navigating the complexities of financial unity within a partnership. Whether you're embarking on this journey as a newly united couple or have been in such a partnership for an extended period,

"Swing the Hammer" provides essential insights into creating and maintaining a harmonious financial relationship.

Brian also recognizes that our responsibility extends beyond our financial health. In a world where financial literacy is often overlooked in our education, "Swing the Hammer" equips us with the knowledge and tools needed to educate the next generation about responsible money management. It's a valuable gift we can pass on to our children, ensuring they start their financial lives with sound practices.

I particularly appreciate the story of Glenn and Connie, a couple who seemed destined for divorce. Through an examination of their relationship with money, Brian illustrates how these techniques effectively saved their marriage and their relationship.

Brian's informal yet direct and inspirational tone will make you feel like you are consulting with a trusted mentor who understands your financial challenges and genuinely wants to offer a path to economic liberation, leading to an improved quality of life. "Swing the Hammer" is more than just a financial planning book; it's a call to action for you. It's an invitation to take charge of your financial health and improve your overall well-being. There's a reason something feels amiss in our lives regarding money. Brian's perspective and guidance on decision-making can be a transformative empowerment process to help us navigate the correct course financially and emotionally.

Whether you're grappling with financial anxiety or seeking to refine your relationship with money, this book can be your road map. It's a prescription for an improved quality of life, with less stress, worries, and depression, ultimately leading to happiness. For many, this will be a transformative journey toward a life free from the debilitating challenges of financial distress. I implore you to delve into the pages of "Swing the Hammer" with an open heart and mind. It is a quick and smooth read. Allow Brian to be your guide on this transformative journey. Your financial health and emotional well-being await your commitment to change.

- Bill

Preface

We've had the privilege of working with clients we greatly admire. What these admirable clients share is a positive relationship with money. They didn't focus solely on their financial statements or monetary assets like big houses, expensive watches, cars, or vacation houses. Instead, they aimed for something deeper: happiness. They sought a balance between accomplishments, contentment, and most importantly, connections with others. These clients were able to separate their feelings from money, which allowed them to spot opportunities, learn from their mistakes, and navigate tough financial times while still finding joy and gratitude in life.

Feeling happy and unburdened by financial worries doesn't necessarily mean you're extremely wealthy in the traditional sense. Some of the richest people we've assisted were actually quite unhappy when we first started working with them. For instance, there was a professional athlete who held bitterness and anger toward those around him. He felt frustrated that his previous achievements seemed to lose their value each year, starting fresh with each new season.

While he had amassed a significant amount of money (with a net worth of over $30 million), he hadn't found a meaningful purpose for his wealth beyond indulgent spending and lending money to friends.

Another client we worked with was a bartender who led a cheerful life, working hard, arriving early, and always wearing a smile. She enjoyed the atmosphere and the music at her workplace, and her friendly demeanor resonated with her customers. Is the bartender extremely wealthy? Not in the traditional sense. However, she had been diligent about saving and investing since her twenties. Now approaching 50 years old, she holds a steady job, earning $73,000 per year, and has built up an Individual Retirement Account (IRA) worth over $1,000,000.

True wealth extends beyond mere financial numbers. It involves cultivating a healthy relationship with money, recognizing that happiness arises from a balance between achievement, contentment, and meaningful connections with others. Detaching emotions from money allows us to seize opportunities, grow from setbacks, and navigate turbulent financial periods while maintaining a sense of joy, gratitude, and community.

This wisdom teaches us that financial well-being isn't solely determined by the size of one's bank account; it's about finding purpose in our resources and making choices that contribute to a fulfilling and contented life. Just as the examples of the professional athlete and the dedicated bartender illustrate, the journey toward financial security and happiness is nuanced, shaped by our decisions, attitudes, and the connections we forge along the way.

The Core Belief:
Money is a tool for happiness.

Just because you have a hammer doesn't mean you're a carpenter.

Just because you have money doesn't mean you're happy.

You need to know how to use the tool in order to achieve the goal.

Swing the hammer and live happily.

We enjoy hearing stories from folks we've assisted before. They lead happier lives by using our simple rules of organization, perspective, and purpose. They've set themselves up to do better at work, get closer to family, and solve community issues.

These clients are proud of their accomplishments and excited about the future.

When COVID-19 and the pandemic shutdowns started, many felt uncertain. Surprisingly, we got messages from happy clients who were relieved to have some extra money set aside for emergencies. Some clients even chose to retire early from their jobs – and they were super excited to share this news with us. They were grateful that they could make this choice because they had been following a consistent but not-too-hard savings plan. Others have passed along these rules to their extended families and gleefully watch sisters and brothers, cousins and in-laws, aunts and uncles climb up out of financial muck and stand fiscally tall. This makes us happy.

The Mission:
To eradicate financial insecurity in America.

We will reference happiness as the antithesis of depression. Here's why: in a seven-year study (2007-2014), the APA, American Psychiatric Association uncovered that the number one disability in the U.S. is depression. The leading non-chemical cause of this depression is financial anxiety. About 75% of adults have significant financial anxiety every month. That is bad. The age ranges for this study were people in their early 20s to retirees. Let's put this in perspective: think of 10 people you work with every day. Are seven or eight of them consumed by financial stresses each month? Think of 10 friends. Think of 10 family members. Think of yourself. Are there 12 moments a year when money worries significantly change your mood? The good news is, 25% are not consumed by money issues. What's the secret? It has little to do with being wealthy or a general sense of monetary apathy. The happy rich value relationships, are grateful, and delight in overcoming the obstacles of life.

The Process:
Organize - Prioritize - Achieve

Our principles aren't new or revolutionary. Instead, they work well because they help clients cut through the noise of media and ads and stay focused. Setting goals is good, but they should be flexible. Talking with a spouse is important, but often it's just words. Budgeting is simple unless it's too strict. Financial security, freedom, and independence are great ideas, but their true meaning is often squandered to excuse lazy habits.

No matter where you are in adulthood, money moves around you like leaves in the windstorm. Knowing what you have, what you owe, what you earn, and what you give is crucial. This starts with being organized. Getting organized might feel like busywork, but it's necessary and magical. People dislike this step because they want to see the big picture before they are finished. They think of this as a financial puzzle. It's not. It's a sculpture, and before we sculpt, we must make the clay.

If they push through it, the next step becomes easier, which is prioritizing. Prioritizing is making a to-do list. Sort through your lists and figure out what needs attention right away to move forward. It can be hard because sometimes, we're not sure where "forward" is yet, making it hard to prioritize, but that's okay. We'll get to goal setting and planning, but first, some financial tidying up. Then, we can see where we stand. Here we'll analyze the different parts of our finances and how they fit together. Figuring out what goals to achieve becomes clear and simple.

Creating a plan is enjoyable, but it involves thinking about "what if" scenarios and checking that things align. Once you get over that part, financial freedom starts growing. Carrying out plans to completion and seeing them work is fulfilling. Sometimes things don't go as planned but being organized and knowing our priorities helps us adjust easily. We can move through the organization process and avoid obstacles to stay on track. Financial success lies in these small steps – having the ability to make a small move and overcome a challenge is not only liberating but also empowering.

Introduction

Talking about money is often thought of as taboo. You will hear phrases like "we don't talk about money." Or "Don't discuss your paycheck." This is amusing and ironic, considering that America is a capitalist society, run and valued by money. Because of this, when we are forced to "money-talk," we stink at it. It is hard for people to separate their financial worth from their worth as an individual. We, almost by default, view, and value the people with lots of money as powerful and important, and vice versa.

As a way for us to detach from these societal norms, this book aims to highlight how we can view money in a positive and healthy way. I want you to be able to evaluate your relationship with money and, in turn, help others who may be having similar experiences.

The seven-year APA study identified that 75% of American adults experience severe anxiety every month over money. Just to be clear, this is not being concerned about saving for college or feeling like you need to make additional mortgage payment changes. This means 75% of Americans feel their world is closing in on them due to finances. And the approach to dealing with it is total denial, or the development of coping mechanisms like anger, authoritarianism in the home, drugs and alcohol, or more impulse spending.

For the last 20-plus years, I've worked with truck drivers and TV stars. Carpenters, schoolteachers, plumbers, and electricians. Some are corporate executives who have made excellent financial choices but are overwhelmed with sadness. We've helped angry grandkids who simply inherited too much wealth too soon. My point in telling you this is, I have seen a lot of family budgets. I've reviewed a wide variety of checking accounts and credit card statements. I've made thousands of balance sheets and cash flow reports. I know their struggles with money, and I know their wins. There are commonalities between different professions, lifestyles, and echelons of net worth.

The president of an insurance company grapples with the same financial behaviors as the stay-at-home mom. Their spending is a coping tool.

The local TV news producer has money motivation problems common to those of a kindergarten teacher. They both constantly compare themselves to others.

The lawyer, who made partner 5 years ago, is frustrated about his income sustainability, much like the woman who is a pharmaceutical rep. Every year, they start at zero - zero sales and zero hours billed. They don't know what the next 12 months will produce as far as income.

A computer programmer fears making investment mistakes in the same way as a commercial plumber. They are both frustrated by the nonlinear nature of the stock market.

I'm accustomed to seeing the patterns of worry and anxiety. Many people feel that the answer is simple: more money. "If I only had more money, less debt, a high income, I'd be fine," is a common mantra. Volume can hide a lot of sins, but the sins are still there. How can money be the problem, and the cause and the solution? We define and assign all three components of financial situations to money. Money is the problem because money is the cause, and money will be the solution.

For example, a couple is having trouble with money. They live paycheck to paycheck. If they had more money, they would have excess dollars each month or a cushion of safety to pay their mortgage, buy food, etc. If they get a raise from their employer, a higher salary, and get more money each month, what happens? Do they use that excess to cushion themselves each month? Do they pay off some extra debt or save a little more? Maybe for a few months. But we all know what eventually happens. That comfort and contentment dissipate over time. And what do they do?

Right, they increase lifestyle. That's the blanket term, "lifestyle," we use for the act of spending your income. They start treating themselves to extras. They accomplished a goal; the raise got them more money – they've righted the financial ship in terms of their monthly woes. They feel good about it and now have a sense of security. That accomplishment and security fuels happiness. Great. But it's short-lived. And soon, they start to increase their lifestyle again. Eating out more, drinking finer wines or whiskies, more digital subscriptions, watches, jewelry, cars, you name it.

Extra conveniences and luxuries are how lifestyle increases. I'm guilty of it. After working all day on Tuesday nights, I hustle home to coach my kid's soccer practice. My wife has worked all day; she coaches our other kid's softball team. When practices are done, a great idea pops into my head: I'll pick up a pizza! I'm paying for convenience – and sometimes laziness. If I am doing this once every few weeks, maybe it's not that bad. But when we pay for convenience out of habit, that's when convenience takes a toll on our finances.

But this example is easy. The message of not spending recklessly is common, and important. There are examples of not spending enough or underspending. Our client, Mary, told us of an epiphany she had organizing and going on a family vacation. She was so nervous about spending "too much" that she and her family drove 20 hours to Florida. Airfare, she thought, was too expensive for such a short trip. Her husband and two kids packed up their Honda CRV and made the trek. Because housing rentals near the beach were four times the cost, Mary booked a motel 8 miles inland. She was feeling very smart and fiscally responsible.

When Saving Money Wastes Money

Mary Mullin planned for one overnight stop on their road trip to Florida. The family would spend ten hours in the car, stop at a cheap motel to sleep, and then 10 more hours of driving the next day. In her mind, just getting to and from their family vacation this way had already saved them hundreds of dollars.

All food for the car ride was fast food.

Mary sensed her plan was unraveling only two hours into their vacation. After a quick stop for drive-thru food, Steve, her husband, was putting the straw into his little Joey's vanilla milkshake. Turning to pass it back, there was a sudden bump in the road. Joey's hand, reaching for his drink, clipped the top plastic lid and smashed it into the Styrofoam cup. A vanilla milkshake explosion covered Joey and Dad, finally landing on the floor, quickly seeping into the car's carpeting. They had to stop again to clean it up.

They made it about halfway to Daytona, Florida, from Houston and found a motel for the night. Because everyone had their own suitcases, all the bags had to be schlepped into the room. Steve was already thinking about how he would have to repack the car the next morning. What Steve didn't imagine was the vile smell created by the soaked in vanilla milkshake in the hot and humid overnight weather of Mobile, Alabama.

This made the second leg of the trek to Daytona quite unpleasant.

Finally arriving at their family vacation spot after spending Saturday and Sunday driving, the Mullin family moved into their rental house, ready for 3 days of beach time and fun. Tuesday would be their first day on the sand. Only packing up what they needed for the beach, they rolled down the windows of the overly vanilla-scented CRV and started the eight-mile drive to sunshine. Mary again started thinking about how smart she was – this eight mile move inland had saved them hundreds of dollars.

The traffic, however, was horrible. They crept along at 5-10-15 miles per hour, reaching the public beach after 45 minutes in the car. Eight miles in 45 minutes was not a blazing pace. Kids and parents, both losing patience with the vacation hiccups so far, tried to make the best of it.

The day went as most beach days go, but the family's ordeal thus far made them extra sensitive to minor mishaps. Parking was rough, but they found a spot about 200 yards from the beach. The beach was crowded, and Steve and Mary were losing energy carrying the two beach bags and four chairs. They set up nearer to the road than the water. Finding a bathroom and food was a whole new mission. Small struggles kept piled on top of each other. The drive home from the beach on day one was quiet. Everyone was questioning, "Does this feel like a vacation?"

Mary noticed the beach houses for rent. She had seen them online and remembered thinking they were too expensive. She watched a family shake out a blanket and casually walk from the beach, up a small flight of stairs, and through a sliding glass door. Minutes later, the beach house mom came back out and sat comfortably on the porch with a book. Her husband followed with drinks. "Maybe those houses are worth the price. They look like they're on vacation!"

For two more days, the Mullins made the pilgrimage to the beach, and then it was time to drive home to Houston. Two days away. Home. It sounded nice. Instead of relaxing on vacation, they were, instead, enduring. Suffering just to make it home. In total, they spent $2,800 to "have a vacation." If they had flown to Daytona, rented a car, and had accommodations on the beach, they would have spent $5,800. They avoided spending $3,000. Great, but for what? Did they build good memories? Did they relax? Did they return home feeling rested and energized? Was the extra savings of $3,000 worth it? Moreover, was the actual spending of $2,800 worth it? Ultimately the big question is: Did they "save" $3,000, or did they waste $2,800? Put another way, did Mary use money as a tool for happiness?

The dualism between spending too much and not spending enough is the struggle to get to know ourselves and what we value. The single word that seems to wrap up all usages of money is happiness.

Don't Eat the Doughnut

Any discussion about our relationship with money must include, preferably start with, a discussion on our relationship with ourselves. We should recognize that money is not merely a reflection of relationships with external factors but also our inner selves.

I have seen two consistent characteristics in clients who live pleasing lives:

1. Self-control and 2. Self-discipline.

Together, these two attributes sculpt the Shakespearean adage to thine own self be true. Conceptually, if you can't be true or honest with yourself, the path of life will be filled with hidden obstacles and surprise attacks. Although life is unpredictable, a dishonest relationship with oneself creates self-inflicted wounds and unforced errors.

Self-control, the ability to resist immediate gratification for long-term goals, is akin to taming a dragon that resides within us. It is the "don't eat the doughnut" rule. In personal finance, easy examples would be saving money instead of spending it.

Self-discipline is the doing of a task despite the lack of desire or drive to do it. This is the "just do it" mentality. Marathon runners train even when it's raining. Parents wash the dishes at night, even though the kids are in bed and all they want to do is sleep. They have the self-control to resist bedtime now and just get the dishes done.

I like the metaphor in adopting a "financial diet." Just as one restricts certain foods to maintain a healthy body, practicing financial self-control requires resisting frivolous or unhealthy spending habits. For instance, curbing impulse purchases or refraining from unnecessary subscriptions can lead to significant savings over time. This disciplined approach enables individuals to allocate funds more efficiently towards investments, education, or personal growth, fostering financial stability and independence.

The honesty that develops from control and

discipline fosters a growth mindset. Embracing a growth mindset allows individuals to view failures as opportunities for learning and improvement rather than dead-ends. Being lazy or sloppy with money is an anchor to our potential.

Never too Late, Ever

We were witness to a great example of this with our clients, Tom Wilkinson. He went through a period of significant financial challenges. Due to some personal and career-oriented setback, Tom showed us tremendous grit. A family member had swindled $3,000,000 from him over 4 years. Tom had also started the process of selling his company to a key employee. His retirement was predicated on his now-gone savings. Without his company, Tom simply could not retire since it was the only source of revenue for him. He was in a financial pickle. Throughout the ordeal, Tom maintained his self-discipline by reframing setbacks as valuable lessons. He had trusted the wrong person, and he had made a promise to his key employee before confirming his plan. He was upset, angry, and felt humiliated – but only for a short period. He took the blame on himself, and at 65 years old he asked himself "now what?"

A simple plan was formed. Tom told the employee of his situation and made a new deal. Together they would run the business for the next 7 years, at which time the employee would pay only $1 for it. Stipulations were set but were simple. Both would draw the same reduced salary. Growth of the company was important and Tom would take any excess of 10% growth as a bonus to recoup his stolen retirement. He also diligently reviewed his personal finances weekly, ensuring his new money was secure. "Blame is pointless at this stage," he said, "I need to do better – I got fat and cocky. Shame on me, but it was a good tuition payment for the lesson learned." He utilized failures as steppingstones towards smarter, controlled, and disciplined financial decisions. Tom retired at 72 and died at age 88 with a net worth of over $8 million. Almost all the principal of that money was earned in his late 60s and early 70s. There is no straight line to success, and happiness is a fleeting state of being.

This seems simple, but it's not easy. Why? From what I've struggled through and what others have confirmed, fear stops us in our tracks on the path to happiness. A potent and primal emotion, fear often emerges as a response to perceived threats or dangers. However, fear can also manifest as a reaction to introspection, unveiling the truth of our current state and revealing the work required to achieve growth and meaningful change. When fear arises from the realization of the effort and work necessary for self-improvement, it acts as a mirror reflecting our true selves back to us.

Confronting fear in the context of personal growth requires a willingness to delve into the depths of our psyche, exploring both our strengths and vulnerabilities. Often, we present a curated version of ourselves to the world, veiling our insecurities and avoiding the discomfort of facing our imperfections. However, when we muster the courage to acknowledge these facets, fear can act as a powerful catalyst for transformation.

Investing in Yourself

Alex is a brilliant accountant and actuary. A man with an unyielding desire for growth, he has always grappled with the fear of public speaking.

Despite this daunting obstacle, Alex carved out a path of success within his company. He cleverly avoided presenting in large meetings or anywhere that required him to stand and talk to more than two people. So, when he was invited to speak of the annual board meeting and present his division accomplishments, he got very nervous. This was an opportunity to showcase his acumen and secure a board position for himself. He could take care of his valuable employees and steer the direction of the company toward greater success.

But the thought of standing before an audience, feeling their eyes drilling into him, magnifying his anxiety – it was too much. How could he get out of it? Could he ask Henry or Grace to speak for him? Could he refuse the invitation? No, deep down he knew that to ascend to greater heights, he must confront and conquer this crippling fear head-on. It was time for Alex to get brutally honest with himself. He craved progress and knew it was time to invest in his transformation.

Driven by his desire to become a confident public communicator, Alex took a bold step and committed his personal funds to seek professional help for public speaking. He spent $8,000 at a private business school, where he embarked on a journey to slay this fear-dragon.

Through diligent effort and consistent practice, Alex gradually desensitized himself to the piercing gazes of the crowd. He learned the art of structuring his talks effectively, realizing that he didn't need to inundate the audience with every minutia his actuary brain could conjure. Instead, he recognized the power of communicating a clear and compelling message, one that resonated with his audience.

By silencing the relentless actuary brain's impulse to cover all bases, Alex allowed space for engagement and curiosity. He discovered that leaving certain minor details unaddressed naturally prompted the audience to ask questions. This dialogue facilitated a deeper connection, positioning Alex as a valuable resource who not only delivered the message but could also address inquiries on the spot.

Alex learned the essence of self-honesty; he confronted his fears. Acknowledging his fear became the catalyst for a path leading to genuine happiness and success. The money he invested wasn't merely a transaction; it was the key that unlocked the door to his communication prowess. Too often we hear the phrase "invest in yourself" but it's a punchline or excuse. Alex really invested in himself. Fix and build. That's how Alex used his money as a tool, but only after an honest and scary self-assessment.

Today, Alex continues to evolve as a communicator, confidently conveying his expertise to captivated audiences. In the pursuit of happiness, we often find ourselves burdened with the fear of overwhelming work and sacrifice. The weight of effort required to make substantial shifts can be paralyzing, hindering our progress on the path to fulfillment. A clear example of this struggle lies in the stories of many young couples grappling with student loan debt, their dreams of financial freedom seemingly out of reach.

<u>Clearing the Clutter and Choosing Intensity</u>

Consider the case of Erica and Alice, a married couple facing the daunting reality of a combined college debt of $130,000. Despite earning a living of $250,000 together, they find themselves entrapped by financial fear, unable to break free from the clutches of debt. It's a common predicament among many, a silent struggle that keeps them from saving and truly enjoying the fruits of their labor.

The turning point came when they faced their financial situation head-on, exploring "what-if" scenarios and seeking a path to escape this cycle. Painful as it was, they confronted their realities: selling the house, considering roommates, adhering to a budget, and meticulously tracking their spending. The singular focus was clear: striving to reach a place where they could save more than they spent.

Questions arose about what truly mattered to them, what brought them happiness, and what they were willing to sacrifice. Through this introspection, they committed to a plan they could believe in, and Erica and Alice embarked on their journey of financial transformation.

Two years later, the results were remarkable. Though still in debt, they managed to halve it and, surprisingly, found themselves happier and more content. It's possible to have debt and be happy – if there is a plan. Strengthened by a deeper bond with each other, they also discovered newfound confidence and resilience within themselves. The process of charting their financial path and committing to it had a profound impact on their lives.

Happiness Formula

Being a happy person may sound trivial, basic, and simplistic. We may like to think of ourselves as hard-chargers, or compassionate, or enlightened. These too are good, but they are merely part of the path towards happiness. Being happy doesn't mean we are looking for euphoria at every moment of the day. Happiness is a balance between three mental states: a sense of achievement, a sense of contentment, and a sense of connection.

If you find yourself in a funk, that is a rut or a state of melancholy, think of your happiness balance and ask if you need more achievement, contentment, or connection. This first step can help create a path to feeling better. It doesn't always take money to get out of this funk, but leveraging your tools, like money, is a great way to get moving. Let's walk through these three concepts.

Achievement can bring a sense of pride, fulfillment, and satisfaction. It can give us a sense of purpose and direction, helping us to feel that our efforts are paying off. This can lead to increased confidence and motivation to continue pursuing our goals and dreams.

However, achievement can also have negative effects. For example, achievement can sometimes lead to a sense of pressure and stress, especially if we are constantly striving to reach the next level or meet expectations. This can lead to burnout and a sense of being overwhelmed, making it difficult to enjoy the rewards of our achievements.

Achievement can sometimes lead to a sense of entitlement and superiority over others. When we feel that we have accomplished something great, it can be easy to believe that we are better than others and that we deserve more than they do. This can lead to a sense of arrogance and a lack of empathy for others, making it difficult to build and maintain healthy relationships.

In addition, the pursuit of achievement can often be driven by external factors, such as the opinions of others or societal expectations. This can lead to a sense of not being true to ourselves, as we may be sacrificing our own values and desires to meet these expectations. This can lead to feelings of unhappiness and dissatisfaction with our lives, even if we have achieved our goals.

Furthermore, the focus on achievement can also lead to a neglect of other important areas of life, such as relationships and self-care. When we are so focused on achieving our goals, it can be easy to neglect our health, relationships, and other important aspects of life. This can lead to a sense of imbalance and unhappiness in our lives, as we may feel that we are missing out on important experiences and connections.

Finally, achievement can also bring a sense of disappointment and unfulfillment, especially if we are unable to meet our goals or if our achievements do not bring the happiness and fulfillment that we expected. This can lead to feelings of failure and a sense of not measuring up, making it difficult to continue pursuing our goals and dreams.

Achievement can bring both positive and negative effects into our lives. While it can bring a sense of pride, fulfillment, and satisfaction, it can also lead to stress, entitlement, and disappointment. It is important to be mindful of the potential negative effects of achievement and to focus on finding a balance between pursuing our goals and taking care of other important areas of our lives. This can help us achieve our goals while experiencing happiness and fulfillment in our lives.

Contentment can be both good and bad for our lives. On the positive side, contentment can bring peace and happiness, allowing us to appreciate what we have and find joy in the present moment. When we are content, we are less likely to be distracted by external factors, such as material possessions or comparisons with others, and more likely to focus on the things that truly matter, such as relationships and personal growth.

However, contentment can also have negative effects. For example, contentment can sometimes lead to complacency and a lack of motivation to grow and improve. When we are content, we may be less likely to challenge ourselves and pursue new experiences, limiting our personal growth and preventing us from reaching our full potential. This can lead to a sense of boredom and unfulfillment in our lives.

Similarly, contentment can sometimes lead to a lack of ambition and a failure to reach our goals. When we are content, we may not feel the need to work as hard or strive for success, which can prevent us from reaching our full potential. This can lead to a sense of regret and disappointment later in life, especially if we are unable to achieve our goals or reach our full potential.

In addition, contentment can sometimes lead to a lack of empathy and compassion for others. When we are content, we may be less likely to see the struggles and challenges of others and more likely to focus on our own happiness and well-being. This can lead to a sense of disconnection and a lack of empathy for others, making it difficult to build and maintain healthy relationships.

Contentment can sometimes lead to a sense of stagnation and a lack of change. When we are content, we may be less likely to take risks or pursue new opportunities, which can prevent us from growing and evolving. This can lead to a sense of being stuck and a lack of progress in our lives.

Finally, contentment can also be fragile and temporary and easily shattered by external events, such as changes in our personal or professional lives. This can lead to feelings of disappointment and unhappiness, especially if our contentment is based on external factors that are beyond our control.

Contentment can be both good and bad for our lives. While it can bring a sense of peace and happiness, it can also lead to complacency, lack of motivation, and a lack of empathy. It is important to strive for a balance between contentment and growth and to focus on finding peace and happiness that is not dependent on external factors. This can help us to maintain a sense of contentment while also pursuing our goals and experiencing personal growth and fulfillment in our lives.

Interpersonal connections, or our personal connections to others, is essential for our well-being, but it also has its pros and cons. On the positive side, personal connection with others provides us with a sense of belonging and community, which is essential for our mental health and happiness. When we have strong personal connections with others, we feel supported, loved, and valued, which helps us navigate life's challenges with greater ease and resilience.

Personal connection with others can provide us with opportunities for growth and learning. When we connect with others, we have the chance to learn from their experiences, perspectives, and knowledge, which can broaden our understanding of the world and help us to grow as individuals. Personal connection with others can also provide us with opportunities to collaborate and work together, which can lead to greater success and fulfillment in our personal and professional lives.

Connection with others can also have negative effects. For example, it can sometimes lead to a sense of vulnerability as we open ourselves up to others and allow them to see our true selves. This can be frightening and difficult, especially if we are not used to connecting with others on a personal level.

Additionally, personal connection with others can sometimes lead to disappointment and conflict, as we may not always agree with others or may not be able to reconcile our differences.

These can be time-consuming and emotionally draining, as it requires us to be fully present and attentive to the needs and feelings of others. This can lead to feelings of exhaustion and burnout, especially if we are not taking care of our own needs and well-being. Additionally, personal connection with others can sometimes lead to feelings of dependency and codependency, as we may become overly focused on our relationships and may not be able to function independently.

It can also lead to a lack of personal boundaries, as we may be too willing to compromise our own needs and wants in order to maintain our relationships. This can lead to feelings of resentment and unhappiness, as we may not be fulfilling our own needs and desires. Another factor can be a lack of privacy and individuality, as we may be too focused on our relationships and may not have the space and time to pursue our own interests and passions.

Personal connection with others is an essential aspect of our lives, but it also has its pros and cons. While it can provide us with a sense of belonging, growth, and learning, it can also lead to feelings of vulnerability, conflict, and exhaustion. It is important to strive for a balance between personal connection and self-care, and to focus on building strong, healthy relationships that are based on mutual respect, trust, and understanding. This can help us to experience the benefits of personal connection while also protecting our well-being and happiness.

Money as Happiness Balancer

It's easy to think of money as an easy button – throw money at a problem and it will be fixed. That certainly can be true, but often we don't realize that money is already in use for a particular solution. Losing weight is a classic example. Do we need to spend money on a new gym, workout equipment, and digital watch to track progress? Maybe, but chances are we need only to put on the sneakers we already own and go for a walk.

Cost Per Wear

Many clients have come to realize that their clothing choices shouldn't be dictated by passing fashion trends. It's perfectly fine to be stylish, but constantly updating your wardrobe every season is impractical. There are staples to wardrobe. Both in men's and women's clothing wardrobes, there are staples we all need. These accommodate outfits for daily life, special occasions, and seasonal (weather related, not fashion seasons) changes.

Basic items like t-shirts, jeans, and underwear form the core of both men's and women's wardrobes. These pieces are designed for comfort, durability, and easy mix-and-match options, making them indispensable for casual wear. Similarly, formal wear, such as suits for men and dresses for women, represents the need for elevated attire in professional or celebratory settings, showcasing the importance of dressing appropriately for special occasions.

Footwear, ranging from athletic shoes to dress shoes, plays a vital role in both genders' wardrobes, providing comfort, protection, and style. Outerwear, such as coats and jackets, addresses the common need to stay warm and dry in various seasons, underlining the importance of functional yet fashionable layering options. Accessories, like belts and watches, are unisex in their ability to enhance an outfit's aesthetic and functionality.

If you buy good quality staple items, you will spend more now, but less over time. It's a matter of cost per wear versus cost to be fashionable. Staples are immune to fashion trends. If double breasted pin-striped suits with extra wide lapels are suddenly back in fashion, should you get one? This is where understanding your happiness balancer starts to help. You're clearly not content because you want to make the purchase. Is the purchase an achievement? Maybe, but likely not. This new purchase will be more of a connection. You want to feel connected to other fashionistas. Is that connection deep and meaningful, or is it superficial?

If your motive is deep and meaningful then by all means, make the purchase. If it's superficial, skip it. Here's what is likely happening – you're not searching for connection but rather contentment. You're not satisfied or grateful (in a wardrobe sense) with your closet. A change is needed, but instead of buying the new fashionable thing, look toward the staples and buy high quality. The economics on buying clothes at a higher price and quality are greatly in your favor. A $300 suit (or jacket, or dress, etc.) will last only 5% of the time a high quality $2,000 purchase will.

There is obviously a big caveat here – just because something is high priced doesn't mean it's high quality.

Do you have the time?

Wristwatches have had a tumultuous history, facing challenges from technological advancements over their relatively short 100-year existence. The "Quartz Crisis" in the late 1960s and 1970s marked a significant turning point. The invention of quartz crystals revolutionized timekeeping, with Japanese watchmakers, especially Seiko, introducing precise and cost-effective quartz watches that disrupted the Swiss watchmaking industry, leading to job losses and bankruptcies. Swiss manufacturers eventually adapted, some by embracing quartz technology and others by emphasizing craftsmanship.

I am a sucker for a nice watch. I like the different styles and movements, and complication displays. I can go deep into talking about the histories of the brands, who took ideas from who, and how the particular models have fared in value of the secondary (used) market. As I was building my collection, (which is a generous way of saying impulse buying) I mostly cared for the look of the watch. I would imagine the scenario in which I would wear a certain one, or even if I knew I was going to meet someone who wore a certain brand I wanted the ability to match that brand or even model number.

My contentment for my watch spending was near zero as I struggled to reach higher and higher with connection. The result was I was not happy with what I had, even though I owned thousands of dollars in watches. Worse, I thought more was the solution. While having lunch with a client, Tony DeLuca, I notice his Rolex Datejust. It was steel, not gold, and on a leather strap. I asked him about it. He said he got it years ago in the army for $500. The bracelet never felt good, so he's had it on a black leather strap ever since, occasionally changing the straps as they wore out. "It's the only watch I have other than a Timex Ironman that I wear for yard work."

Tony was an oil executive and had plenty of money. Oh, the collection he could build! But he had just the two watches. One "beater watch" for yard work and one for everything else. What an investment, 40-45 year old watch with a cost basis of $500 that is now worth about $10,000. Does he know the value? "Do you know those have increased in price quite a bit?"

"That's a value to someone else. I paid $500, and it looks nice. The real cost is the maintenance and leather straps. I buy this watch every few years in maintenance. Five years ago, its service was $500, five years from now, it's $500, and so on. It's fine. It's my watch, problem solved. I can't understand the people that have 40-50 watches." I got very quiet.

This interaction stuck with me for a while. Over time I started to evaluate contentment over connection. I realized I could still connect by keeping up with the watch world and releases, but I didn't have to own everything. I can appreciate great watches and I don't have to be burdened by the need to own them all. I've pared my collection back to two dress watches, two casual, one Timex Ironman.

Renting your Kitchen

Many of us can relate to the struggle of cluttered kitchen cabinets filled with a plethora of rarely used culinary gadgets. Personally, as someone who spends a significant amount of time in the kitchen, I find myself primarily relying on just a single pan, a solitary pot, and a lone cast iron skillet. Surprisingly, amidst my culinary arsenal, I've amassed six skillets, yet I find myself using only one. The same pattern emerges with my chef knives; I faithfully employ just one while possessing an overwhelming collection.

The question that lingers is, why do I continue to accumulate these seemingly unnecessary items? The answer lies in understanding the underlying impulse behind these acquisitions. I've come to realize that the fleeting joy of acquiring these new kitchen tools often overshadows the enduring contentment that should derive from the tools I already possess. It's a puzzling phenomenon, a cycle of impulse buying driven by the allure of novelty rather than practical necessity.

The solution to this conundrum lies in reshaping my approach to spending money. Instead of succumbing to the temptation of acquiring new gadgets, I can redirect my resources towards enhancing the functionality and longevity of the items I already own. For instance, investing in a high-quality sharpening stone or maintenance system can work wonders. An old knife, skillfully sharpened and restored, can evoke just as much satisfaction as a brand-new, razor-sharp counterpart.

In essence, it's a shift from the chase for new possessions to a focus on maximizing the value and utility of what I already have. By doing so, not only can I declutter my kitchen and reduce wasteful spending, but I can also savor the enduring delight that comes from mastering the art of maintaining and cherishing the tools of my culinary trade. This shift in mindset is not only applicable to the kitchen but can also be extended to various aspects of life, emphasizing the importance of contentment and the wise use of resources.

Money Math

In all areas of finance, there's a fundamental principle that lies at the heart of understanding the true worth of a dollar—The Time Value of Money (TVM). Though it might sound like an awkward phrase, it holds the key to unlocking the dynamic nature of money and the significance of its timing.

At its essence, the time value of money underscores the concept that a dollar today is not equivalent to a dollar in the future. Money's value isn't merely confined to the face value of a note or coin; it is the gateway to goods, services, and opportunities—a medium of exchange. As we will discuss later in our section about kids and money, money is a method of convenient exchange of value. For this fourth dimension, Time itself comprises three essential components: the past, the present, and the future. Looking back, assets acquired decades ago may have significantly appreciated, underscoring the impact of time on value.

A property bought in 1950 for $30,000 could be worth anywhere from $120,000 to $900,000 today, thanks to 2-5% annual increases. Similarly, the cost of a new Ford truck in 1980 at $6,000 has surged to around $50,000 new today. Even salaries bear the mark of time's touch; the average U.S. salary in 1990 was $30,000, and in 2020, it has risen to $70,000.

The core tenet of TVM recognizes that money has the potential to grow or be invested, yielding returns over time. A dollar received today carries the prospect of being invested, fostering the possibility of growing into a larger sum in the future. Conversely, a dollar received in the future is less valuable since it might have been invested and grown during the waiting period. This profound insight helps individuals make informed financial decisions and assess the true value of various options.

Let's delve deeper into some key components and applications of the time value of money in personal finance, turning it into a powerful tool in your financial arsenal.

Future Value (FV): Imagine peering into the crystal ball of finance to foresee the value of an investment or a sum of money at a specific future date—that's future value. It considers the initial principal, the interest rate, and the time period over which the investment grows. Armed with future value knowledge, you can better assess the potential growth of your investments and make decisions with heightened clarity and foresight.

Present Value (PV): Ever wondered about the worth of a future cash flow in today's terms? That's where present value comes into play. It signifies the current value of an expected future cash flow, taking into account factors such as interest rates and time. Present value calculations come in handy when determining the worth of future cash flows, like assessing retirement savings or annuities.

Compound Interest: Meet the magician of money growth—compound interest. This financial wizardry ensures that interest isn't confined to the initial principal; it accrues on any accumulated interest too. As a result, money grows exponentially over time. Early investments are akin to planting seeds of wealth, as they can flourish into significant sums in the long run through the magic of compounding.

Inflation: Every financial journey involves a dance with inflation—a gradual increase in prices over time. This phenomenon chips away at the purchasing power of money, eroding its value. Hence, the time value of money urges us to consider inflation when evaluating the future value of investments or setting financial goals. Factoring in inflation allows us to contextualize money's worth across time.

Opportunity Cost: The choices we make in our financial endeavors carry with them the concept of opportunity cost—the potential return or benefit sacrificed by choosing one option over another. In the world of personal finance, understanding opportunity cost helps us evaluate and compare different financial choices. By weighing the potential returns of different options, we can navigate the labyrinth of financial decision-making with more clarity and wisdom.

Discounting: Picture yourself with a financial time machine capable of calculating the present value of future cash flows. That's the magic of discounting. It incorporates the time value of money by accounting for interest rates or the discount rate. Discounting helps assess the current worth of future income or cash flows, empowering us to make informed decisions and financial projections.

Why do we need to understand these terms? Time is a factor when dealing with money. My partner, Iris, is a former mortgage expert and helped Rana and Neil Amolgaya understand time and the value of it while explaining how mortgages work. Rana and Neil dreamt of owning a cozy home where they could create beautiful memories together. However, the world of mortgages seemed like an intimidating maze to navigate.

Straight Lines Aren't Straight Forward

They sipped coffee in our office, and Iris offered her wisdom. "Imagine a mortgage as a timeline – as a journey through time," Iris began. "It helps us understand how money changes in value over time."

She pulled out a piece of paper and drew a straight line. "This is our timeline," she said. "On the left side, we have the present, and on the right side, we have the future."

Iris introduced the concept of compounding by explaining that money can grow over time with interest. She used a simple example of a savings account to illustrate this point.

"If you deposit $1,000 into a savings account

with an annual interest rate of 5%, the money will grow each year," she explained. "At the end of the first year, you'll have $1,000 + 5% of $1,000, which is $1,050. Then, the next year, the interest will be calculated on $1,050, not just the original $1,000." Rana and Neil nodded, clearly seeing the effects of compounding.

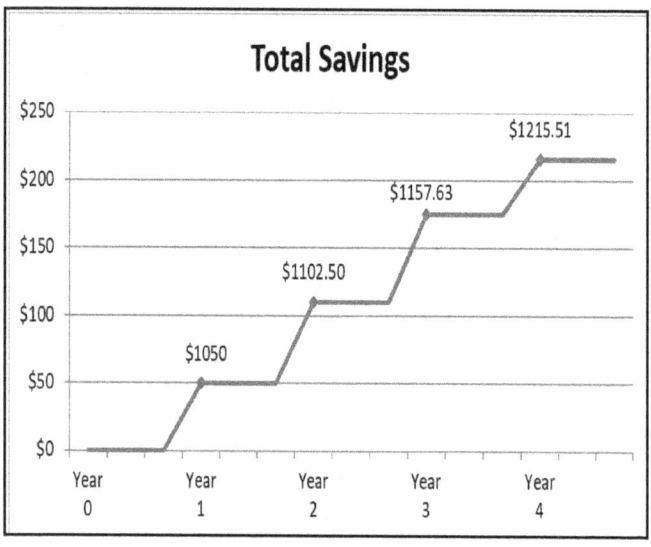

"Now, let's apply the concept of compounding to a mortgage," Iris continued. "A mortgage is a loan you take from a lender to buy a home. You pay back the loan over time, usually with interest."

She drew another timeline, but this time, it represented a 30-year mortgage for a $250,000 home with a fixed interest rate of 4%.

"Here, the left side is the present, and the right side represents the future," she said. "Each year, you'll make mortgage payments, which will reduce your loan balance. Simultaneously, the interest will accumulate on the remaining balance, so your debt will decrease over time." Rana and Neil followed along, grasping the concept.

"Now, let's talk about the time value of money," Iris said with a gleam in her eye. "The time value of money is the idea that money in the future is worth less than money in the present."

She explained that this was because money has the potential to grow over time due to investment opportunities or inflation. Therefore, $100 today is worth more than $100 in the future.

"To calculate the present value of money, you use the formula: Present Value (PV) = Future Value (FV) / (1 + Interest Rate (i)) ^ Number of Years (n)," she explained. It looks like this…" She wrote the following formula on the whiteboard:

$FV = PV(1+i)^n$

Iris showed them how to apply the formula to their mortgage example. "After 30 years, you'll have paid a total of $429,674, which includes $179,674 in interest on top of the original $250,000," she said.

She then introduced the concept of present value, which involves determining the worth of a future sum in today's terms.

Iris showed them how they could calculate the present value of their mortgage payments to understand how much they'd need to invest today to have enough to pay off the mortgage in 30 years. Moreover, they got a lesson on how to use a financial calculator on their phones! The couple felt powerful and soon began to produce what-if scenarios by themselves.

When they found a house they liked, Rana and Neil gave us a presentation on why they could afford it, proudly time-lining out the effects of their financial situation and accurately calculating home equity and debt service.

Now, let's explore the practical applications of understanding the time value of money in various personal finance scenarios, enabling you to navigate the ebb and flow of your financial landscape confidently.

In Retirement Planning: The symphony of retirement planning requires the harmonious synchronization of financial instruments. By starting to save and invest early, individuals can benefit from the crescendo of compounding, building their retirement funds significantly over time. This foresight enables them to grasp the future value of investments and anticipate the impact of inflation—essential notes in composing a financially comfortable retirement.

For Loan Repayment: The time value of money shines a spotlight on the intricacies of loan repayment. When taking out a loan, understanding the concept of time value of money helps us calculate the total amount paid back, encompassing both the principal and interest. Armed with this knowledge, we can assess the true cost of borrowing and make well-informed decisions regarding our debt obligations.

Making Investment Decisions: The grand overture of investment decisions can be daunting, but with the time value of money as your conductor, you can navigate with ease. Evaluating the future value and potential returns of different investment options empowers you to make astute choices. By comparing the present value of investments with the expected future value, you can assess which investments offer the most favorable risk-return profile.

As you grasp the essence of TVM, you'll find yourself gracefully shifting between the rhythm of urgency and patience in regard to your money.

In moments of immediacy, where swift action

is essential, the time value of money equips you to respond with informed precision. Picture this: your refrigerator breaks, and you're faced with a culinary conundrum—how can you save the food for your big party in four days? The time value of money whispers in your ear, guiding you to analyze the best course of action for your financial well-being. This was the situation for a client several years ago.

Knowing Purpose and Value Helps in Choosing the Right Tool

Jack and Sarah Teno were known for their charming country farmhouse and warm hospitality. They were especially fond of hosting dinner parties on Saturday nights, where friends and neighbors would gather to enjoy good food and each other's company.

It's Tuesday, early evening, and with excitement in the air, Jack and Sarah set out to prepare for their upcoming dinner party. They made a comprehensive shopping list and ventured into town to procure all the necessary ingredients for their culinary masterpiece. The weekly pop-up farmer's market was abuzz with fresh produce, and the aroma of artisanal bread filled the air. As they made their purchases, Sarah couldn't help but imagine the joyous faces of their guests as they savored the delightful feast.

As they returned home, bags full of goodies in hand, they felt a sense of accomplishment. However, little did they know that their world was about to be thrown into disarray. Late on Tuesday evening, they retired to bed, blissfully unaware of the impending storm.

Wednesday morning dawned with bright promise, but the Tenos awoke much later than usual, startled by the lack of the familiar alarm clock chime. There must have been a power outage overnight, causing their alarms to fail. Frantically, they jumped out of bed, realizing they were running late for work.

In a hurry to get going, they prepared their cups of coffee to go and went to the fridge for milk. But as they opened the door, their hearts sank. The refrigerator was lifeless, its light extinguished, and its contents in jeopardy. Panic surged through Jack and Sarah as they realized the potential catastrophe before them.

Their minds raced as they thought about the party's food spoiling and the farmer's market wouldn't be back until next week. They had no access to replace the food they had already bought. Rushed out the door, leaving trays of ice in the fridge, they resolved to find a solution.

With each passing minute, their worry intensified. The clock was ticking, and the party was only a few days away. They considered the repair option, but after a call to the local repair service, they were informed that the necessary parts wouldn't be available until after the party.

Desperate for alternatives, they called friends and family, hoping someone might lend them space in their refrigerator. Unfortunately, luck was not on their side, as everyone was either away or already using all the available space.

Time was slipping away, and they were left with no choice but to explore the possibility of buying a new refrigerator. They discovered a floor model that was available for immediate delivery, but there was a catch - it didn't qualify for free financing. The cost was $2400, and they had to pay in cash.

Jack and Sarah sat down together, calculating the options. On one hand, they could pay now and have the refrigerator delivered tomorrow, ensuring their food would be safe and fresh for the party. On the other hand, they could opt for the financing plan and pay $100 per month for 24 months, but the delivery would be delayed until next week.

Time suddenly had a monetary value, and the couple had to decide if it was worth paying the full amount now to avoid potential losses and added stress. They knew they had worked hard for their money, and the idea of spending it all at once weighed heavily on their minds.

After much contemplation, they arrived at a decision that surprised even them. They realized that time had an intangible cost beyond just money. The value of ensuring a successful dinner party, the joy of sharing delicious food with friends, and the peace of mind that came with resolving the issue outweighed the financial implications.

Jack and Sarah chose to pay in cash and have the refrigerator delivered the next day. It was a bold move, but as they sat back and reflected on their choice, they knew they had made the right decision. Time was precious, and sometimes, spending money upfront was the most prudent investment.

As the Saturday night dinner party arrived, their home was filled with laughter, chatter, and the aroma of mouthwatering dishes. Their guests were delighted with the sumptuous feast and appreciated the hospitality that the Tenos were known for.

In the end, it wasn't just about the refrigerator or the dinner party. It was a lesson in understanding the value of time and the hidden costs that accompanied it. Jack and Sarah had learned that sometimes, the most prudent financial decision was not always the one that appeared the most cost-effective on the surface.

The Fridge Dilemma became a tale often recounted in their tight-knit community, not just as a dinner party story but as a reminder of the intangible worth of time and the value of making decisions that truly mattered in the grander scheme of life.

Buckets of Cash

Every so often, I will get a phone call from someone who asks: "I have an IRA, and I just want to know – is that a good investment?" At first, the question confused me because of its puzzling nature. IRAs are accounts that hold types of investments; they are not investments themselves.

My reaction was akin to someone asking me if they have a healthy diet since they have a refrigerator. I don't know – what's in the refrigerator? Even then, we can't know since there are many other factors to consider. In this chapter, let's delve into the basic types of financial accounts, which I like to think of as buckets.

The first question to ask is about the taxation of the account. There are two main ways an account (or bucket of your money) is taxed. 1. Unearned growth over the previous taxable year and 2. Upon removal of money from an account. Unearned income, which I call growth, is money that your account received despite any effort on your part. The simplest example is a savings account at a bank. The bank may credit your account 2% on the amount you have with them per year. If you have $10,000 in the savings account on January 1st and never withdraw or contribute to that account during the year, the bank will add $200 to your account. This is the theory, but of course, it is more complicated. Each month, they will add 1/12 of 2% of the account value or 0.1667%.

This permits more accuracy in fluctuation of account values.

After a year, you suddenly have an extra $200. Depending on the type of account, the government might tax you. A savings account is a taxable account. You owe a tax. If you had this in an IRA, it would not be taxed that following year. This account is nontaxable on growth. But the government wants its tax dollars, so they will tax IRA withdrawals (sometimes referred to as distributions). This kind of money is called "qualified money." Though it is not defined as such, I think of this money as "qualified to grow tax-free."

There are three moments or incidences that trigger taxation of accounts: 1. Before you contribute (such as a ROTH IRA), 2. Upon valuation of unearned income (like your savings accounts), and 3. When you withdraw money from the account (as in traditional IRAs). A ROTH IRA is one that is qualified, but the government gets its tax dollars right away. You pay taxes on your income, then you contribute to your ROTH IRA with what is called after-tax income. The benefit here is no tax is due when you withdraw your money.

There is no "best account" to have, but rather, you should have a variety of accounts that meet your needs. Just like you should have a variety of food in the refrigerator or tools in your toolbox.

The type of account also has an ownership designation. Ownership means control, and it also can make transfer of control easier upon the death of the original account owner. A quick summary follows.

Individual Account (Sole Ownership): This is the most straightforward type of ownership. The account is owned and operated by a single individual. They have complete control over the account and its assets.

Joint Account: A joint account is owned by two or more individuals, often with rights of survivorship. This means that if one account holder passes away, the remaining account holder(s) inherit the assets without going through probate.

Tenants in Common: This is similar to a joint account, but with one significant difference. Each account holder has a specified percentage ownership of the account, and in the event of the death of one account holder, their share of the account passes to their heirs through the probate process.

Community Property: This type of ownership is recognized in some states within the United States and applies to married couples. It defines all property acquired during the marriage as being equally owned by both spouses, including financial accounts.

Trust Account: A trust account is held by a trustee on behalf of one or more beneficiaries. The trustee manages and administers the account according to the terms and conditions set forth in the trust agreement.

Custodial Account: This type of account is set up for the benefit of a minor, with an adult custodian managing the account until the minor reaches the age of majority.

Corporation or Business Account: This type of account is owned by a corporation or a business entity rather than an individual. The account is operated according to the business's structure and with the authorization of the company's officers or representatives.

Partnership Account: Owned by two or more partners, this type of account is typically used for partnerships or joint ventures, with each partner having specified rights and responsibilities.

IRA (Individual Retirement Account) or 401(k) Account: These accounts are specific retirement savings accounts and have unique ownership rules and tax benefits.

Estate Account: This type of account is set up to manage the assets of a deceased person's estate during the probate process.

Let's summarize: So far, accounts or buckets can be qualified or non-qualified. This attribute signifies if the investments inside the bucket (your money or stocks or bonds) grow tax-free. The government wants its tax dollars, and depending on the type of account, you may pay tax at the beginning of the contribution's life, while money is growing, or later when you withdraw the money. Lastly, accounts have owners, which means control. Control can be what assets get in, are taken out, withdrawn, moved, etc. The ownership type also helps understand what happens in the event of death of the original owner.

It is not unusual to have various types of accounts with different ownership designations. Your financial plan will dictate what's best. If you contribute all your money to a 401(k), do you still have enough left over to buy food?" The accounts you open form the financial structure in which you live. Like a home, you may tear down a section or replace it with another. As your needs change in life, additions and subtraction of accounts will occur.

There is no one-way or singular combination of accounts to have in order to build your financial structure. Here's a basic blueprint for what others do.

No account: Cash in-house $1,000-$5,000. This is not to pay the pizza guy; this is strictly an unforeseen need for cash on hand. Power outages can shut down ATMs and close banks. You may lose access to money in those institutions for a week or two. Having cash in small bills (1s, 5s, 10s, 20s) can help you operate in case of emergency.

1. Checking Account One (Joint): This acts as the

operating account for the family.

Bills are paid out of this account and money earned via salary is deposited here.

2. Savings Account One (Joint): The account is commonly referred to as an emergency fund. The emergency fund starts as 3 months of living expenses: food, mortgage, car payments, etc. As the couple matures and makes more money, it grows to 6-8 months. During retirement (and sometimes pre-retirement), this account typically grows to 1-2 years of cash. The purpose of this account is to provide a runway of time for financial conditions to improve. If you lose your job or have a sudden big expense, you won't have to make dramatic lifestyle changes immediately.

3. Checking Accounts Two and Three (Joint): The second and third checking accounts are for each spouse individually. This is the "allowance" or blow-it money. Though the accounts are jointly owned, each spouse gets to decide what happens with that money. Morning coffees and doughnuts, gifts, special clothing, or even just save it.

4. Savings Account Two (Joint): This account is for short to medium-term goals in which a large slug

of money is needed. It gets funded by the operating account or even as a direct deposit from paychecks. Typical things this account is used for are new home purchases, home improvements, new cars or boats, annual vacations, milestone events, major appliances, etc.

5. Qualified Retirement Plan: These hold stocks, bonds, mutual funds, and ETF (Exchange Traded Funds). There are many types of qualified plans, and this can get confusing. Through an employer, you will likely get only one or two options. For example, if you work for a very large corporation, you may get a choice of Roth 401(k) or a Traditional 401(k). There are many, though: 457(b), 403(b), Straight PSP, SEP IRA, Traditional IRA, CBAs, DBA, Pension, PSP… it's a big list. The specific operation of the account types and their various attributes could, and have, fill an entire textbook. For you, it is important to know this. There are two types of qualified retirement accounts: 1. Defined Benefit and 2. Defined Contribution. Defined benefit plans and defined contribution plans are two distinct types of employer-sponsored retirement arrangements. In a defined benefit plan, retirees are assured a predetermined retirement benefit, calculated using variables such as salary and ten-

ure. Employers bear the investment risks and financial obligations to fulfill the promised benefits. On the other hand, in defined contribution plans, participants are responsible for making contributions from their income, often matched by employers, and the retirement benefit is determined by the accumulated contributions and the investment performance of the chosen assets. This fundamental difference underscores the varying levels of financial security and control experienced by participants within these two plan categories.

6. Brokerage Investment Account (Joint): Like a qualified plan, brokerage accounts (or investment accounts) hold stocks, bonds, ETFs, and mutual funds. These are used for excess savings and investing. Retirement account funds cannot be withdrawn until age 59 ½ without penalty. These funds are available for use within 1-3 days of need. All growth is taxed each year, but you can also contribute as much as you like to these accounts, whereas retirement accounts have various and strict limits on total annual contributions.

The total value of all these account types makes up your "portfolio of wealth" and can be shown on the asset side of your balance sheet, which we discussed earlier.

As time goes by, you may find a need to add a 527 plan for college savings, create a trust fund, or make a corporate account for your budding real estate portfolio cash management. The number and structure of accounts are endless and can be tailored to fit your needs.

Buckets of Money: Account Structures

Michael Chen and Andrea Morris-Chen were in their early 30s when we first met them. Michael worked as an engineer at Raytheon, a leading aerospace technology company, while Andrea was an entrepreneur at heart and wanted to buy, run, and grow a small manufacturing business. The type of manufacturing was less important to her, but she had degrees in engineering and metallurgy. When they first crossed paths with a financial planning firm, their financial situation was a mix of potential and challenges. They were both smart, motivated, and had a good sense of teamwork within their marriage.

At that time, Michael was the sole breadwinner, drawing a steady income from his engineering job. On the other hand, Andrea was actively seeking a small business to buy, but their savings didn't allow them much for a purchase price. They had a makeshift plan of buying a company for about $1,000,000 using a loan to fund the majority of the purchase price.

With a shared vision for their future, the couple had saved $120,000, which was in a single checking account. They also had an additional $8,000 in a savings account. This financial setup, as financial planners referred to it, was their "mechanics of money flow." It was straightforward but needed adjustment to align with their ambitions. Both accounts were in Michael's name only.

Unfortunately, Andrea got tired of the constant scouring for potential businesses. She started to look for a steady source of income and took a job at Kaman Corp., another aerospace company. Her desire didn't wane completely for business of her own; she just needed a break from the 2-year grind of business hunting.

During this time and realizing the need for a more strategic approach, we recommended a revamped account structure. We suggested a new money flow: 3 checking accounts, 2 savings accounts, and Michael's 401(k). Since Andrea had just started at Kaman, she was not yet eligible to participate in the 401(k) there.

We introduced the new accounts: one joint "family account" and two individual accounts for personal allowances. The joint account would be the centerpiece for managing their shared expenses. It would be how they operated day-to-day expenses. Both salaries would be directly deposited into the family checking account. From there, each of them would get an allowance transferred into a personal checking account for their individual use. Michael would get $250 per month put into his checking account, which could be used for anything – beers with the guys, new sunglasses, etc. Likewise, Andrea would get $250 deposited into her personal checking account. She could save it, spend it – just like Michael. Car detailing, Starbucks coffee treats, fancy sushi dinners with her sister, all okay with her allowance.

Next, we introduced the purpose of the 2 savings accounts. The first one was called the emergency fund. This was to pay for unexpected, unplanned expenses – a money cushion. If they had sudden medical bills or job loss, this account was there to give them a runway to outlast an unforeseen financial hardship. The typical rubric is 3-6 months of expenses in cash. Six months of expenses for them was about $32,000.

The last account we suggested was a goal account. The goal was to buy a business. Excess money, that is money left over from maxing out Michael's 401(k), paying the family bills, ensuring $32,000 was in the emergency fund, and each spouse getting their allowance, was to be put into this second savings account. This was the "Andrea's Buy a Business Savings Account." They liked the idea and wanted to start:

Current Structure	Michael Checking $120,000 Michael Savings $8,000 Total $128,000
New Structure	Family Checking $10,000 Michael Checking $250 Andrea Checking $250 Family Emergency Saving $32,000 Buy a Business Saving $85,500 Total.......................................$128,000

They dove in headfirst with the plan, feeling great about having a purpose for the money. They opened and funded the accounts as prescribed and enjoyed the new structure. But that's not the whole story. Eventually, both Andrea and Michael started to (somewhat accidentally) save money in their individual checking accounts. When they accumulated over $1,000, they would just dump the excess into the Buy a Business account. Within a year, they were shocked to find this account back at $120,000. The next year, it was over $200,000. Soon, Andrea started to realize that the extra money meant she could entertain the idea of buying a bigger, more established business.

In the third year of the new structure, and with $250,000, Andrea bought a small spring manufacturing company in Waterbury, Connecticut. It has 17 employees, gross sales of $780,000 per annum, and big potential in some untapped markets. She works hard, long, and nerve-racking hours and loves it. In a meeting with them after a year of ownership, Andrea shared this with us:

"If we had not changed something as simple as the structure of our accounts, we'd still only have $120,000 saved up. I'd probably have a new car, and Michael would have probably bought a boat. In three years, we have more savings, two new cars, and two boats. I can't believe account structure would be so important."

The value of account structure is 1. Simplicity of Understanding, and 2. Focused Purpose. A complex plan works only on paper, constantly under attack by real-world dynamics. Purpose creates motivation. Without it, we're just walking down a road to an unknown destination and eventually decide that the struggle isn't worth the effort.

OPA! Working Freedom

In the land of liberty and opportunity, we often take pride in the word "freedom," yet it's true absence can elude us. America's abundance of freedom sometimes disguises the invisible chains we put on ourselves. Yes, we may reside in a land of freedom, but to truly experience financial freedom, we must embrace the power of organization.

Many of us go through life with vague hopes, hoping our financial behaviors will somehow lead us to a secure future. However, hope alone cannot grant us the freedom we desire. True liberation lies in understanding our financial landscape with clarity and precision.

To reach genuine financial freedom, we must shatter the illusions we create and confront the reality of our money, debts, opportunities, and obligations. As uncomfortable as it may be, we must face the shocking truth of what we are doing with our finances and what our money is truly funding.

The path to illumination begins with the best tools at our disposal: the cash flow report and balance sheet. The cash flow report vividly depicts money inflow and outflow, while the balance sheet assesses our financial worth, reflecting the value of our assets and liabilities.

Imagine budgets as a form of cash flow reports. They offer a glimpse into the money coming in and the avenues through which it flows out of our lives. On the other hand, balance sheets tell the story of our net worth, painting a picture of our financial standing—positive or negative.

It's essential to check our egos at the door and face the numbers without making excuses. A wise adage with our clients' echoes, "Don't tell me what you value, show me your cash flow and balance sheet, and I'll tell you." Harsh but honest, this approach uncovers our true financial priorities.

Money Flow: The Ins and Outs

Take the story of Billy Geold, a professional athlete and client of ours. Billy spoke fervently about his passion for a college education for his kids. Admirable as it may be the truth lay in his financial actions. A deeper look revealed that he spent $3,000 per month on wine but only allocated $300 per month to his kids' college savings. A revelation that bruised his ego, but instead of becoming defensive, he embraced honesty and exclaimed, "You're right. Got it."

It is one thing to proclaim our beliefs, but the budget reflects our true commitments. Now, not everyone finds spreadsheets and cash flow statements to be a walk in the park. To address this, we've developed a simplified system—the HOGG Method. This acronym categorizes the four relationships we have with money, making financial clarity attainable for all.

HOGG Method:
- Have: Things you have, known as "assets" (Cars, House, and Money).
- Owe: Things you owe, termed "liabilities" (Borrowed, Promised - Loans & Rents).
- Get: Collection of pay, including Salary, Rents, Royalties, Commission, and Bonus.
- Give: What you give or spend, with a preference

for "give" as it signifies a choice.

The beauty of the HOGG Method lies in its simplicity, empowering us to make clear-cut choices. By adopting this approach, we gain profound insights into where we experience freedom and where we unknowingly shackle ourselves.

The path to true financial freedom starts with introspection and ends with empowering choices. Embrace the HOGG Method and navigate your financial landscape with confidence. With this newfound clarity, you'll be on the fast track to financial liberation, where true freedom awaits you.

The important first step to making progress lies in organization and prioritization. As we set sail towards our dreams and aspirations, we encounter areas of unknowns and challenges, but these shouldn't deter us. Instead, they signal the need to prioritize and chart a course that leads us to success.

Consider the concept of prioritizing as setting goals and listing tasks, like plotting way-points on a sailing trip. When navigating through life, we must continually ask ourselves, "What is important now?" If we need to sail to the other side of an island, we will need to pass through several way-points. If we take a direct bearing on the destination, we will run aground – into the island itself. What is our first way-point? Plot it. We can certainly project out a few points or even a whole journey, but we must remember that we won't have all the data for every point. There may be a shipwreck to avoid or a convoy of tankers to sail around. What is next needed to continue our journey?

In financial planning, goals serve as desired end states, much like way-points on a boating expedition. While conventional wisdom suggests specific goals with deadlines, successful individuals often embrace a more fluid approach. Goals, like way-points, can be adjusted as we sail through the changing tides of life.

Imagine yourself at the helm of a boat, charting a course towards a distant destination. Each way-point represents a milestone, a marker guiding you to your ultimate goal. As you sail towards these way-points, you may find that the journey is not always linear. You might make small adjustments or deviate slightly to adapt to shifting circumstances or avoid obstacles in your path.

Similarly, financial goals act as way-points, guiding us on our journey to a brighter future. At a certain age, you might envision owning a beach house or saving a specific amount of money. Along the way, you may need to make course corrections or add checkpoints to stay on track. These way-points provide a sense of direction and purpose, ensuring you remain steadfast even when the seas of life become rough.

Having clear goals or end states in mind before setting sail helps you chart a more precise path. However, if the destination seems distant or uncertain, it's perfectly fine to start with shorter-term goals. As you embark on the journey towards these more immediate goals, the bigger picture may reveal itself, leading you to discover your broader mission.

For those struggling to define shorter-term goals, general goals can provide direction. By keeping multiple options open and remaining flexible, you can adapt to changing conditions while still moving forward.

Visualization is a powerful tool for goal setting. When you can vividly see the end state, you gain clarity about the goal and the path to reach it. Visualized goals often fall into three categories:

1. Self-Increase Goals: These focus on enhancing abilities, skills, knowledge, and relationships. Whether it's learning a new language, earning educational degrees, or building strong alliances, self-increasing goals fuel personal growth and development.

2. Compound Ordering: By staging tasks in a

logical sequence, you make larger, daunting tasks more manageable. Just like clearing the room before painting, breaking down complex objectives into smaller steps eases the journey and enhances productivity.

3. Motivational Snowball: Harness the excitement and momentum from one achievement to propel you towards accomplishing surrounding tasks. The satisfaction of saving for a family trip may inspire you to eat out less or pack lunches, setting off a chain reaction of positive actions.

Picture yourself as the captain of your financial ship, using way-points as guideposts to navigate the waters of life. By setting priorities, visualizing goals, and embracing flexibility, you can confidently sail towards financial freedom, all the while knowing that each step brings you closer to the destination of your dreams. So, set your course, hoist the sails, and let the winds of motivation carry you to success!

Planning, organizing, and prioritizing can lead us to a state of blissful productivity where facts align, and changes fall into place. But to achieve our goals, we must navigate through the way-points. We must take that pivotal step—action. Planning without action leads to stagnant waters, and stagnation breeds discontent.

Taking action may appear daunting at first, but it becomes second nature with practice. Effort is the fuel that powers the engine of action. Just like doing push-ups, the more we do them, the easier they become. There will be days when we falter, and that's alright. Keep going, persist, and soon enough, success will grace us with its presence.

Finding the motivation can be a battle. Jon Snow, an assistant field manager for the local utility company, found having clarity of goals coupled with a chosen intensity level of effort was his secret formula for self-motivation. Leading a 35-person crew without the ability to influence their pay scale or bonuses, Jon relied on clear project visions and intense execution plans to inspire his team. The goal became about the value to thousands of fellow residents and how they could hold their heads high about doing high-quality work. The greater purpose was pushed. Jon involved them at decision crossroads: "We can finish this portion, and it might be good enough for 10 years, or we can push harder now and make it last for 100 years – what do you guys think?" His crew chose greatness.

In our pursuit of greatness, no matter the intensity, the light we cast has shadows. Procrastination lurks. Self-discipline is our ally, urging us to persist despite fleeting motivation. Through action, we continue to propel ourselves forward, reaching beyond plateaus and embracing growth.

Arambhashura—being a hero in the start—is a familiar dance for many. Initiating a goal with fervor, only to witness the intensity wane over time. To remain in motion, to keep the fire of motivation burning, we must cultivate self-discipline and resilience. As we keep moving, we unveil the treasures that lie beyond each horizon, ensuring our journey is one of progress and accomplishment.

The bridge from planning to achievement lies in action. It is the currency of change and the catalyst for transformation. Embrace the possibility of learning, persist through moments of uncertainty, and let self-discipline be your guiding star. As you take action, the dance of success will lead you to remarkable heights, and the way-points of your dreams will become steppingstones to a life of fulfillment and growth. So, set sail with purpose, knowing that action is the wind that propels you towards greatness.

Risk of Life

Life is full of risks. Some risks have dire consequences, and others tame. To make progress through achievement, there needs to be, by necessity, an element of risk. Some risks we bear, some we reduce, and some we can avoid. We can also transfer the risk to someone or something else. When we transfer risk, typically, we are referring to insurance. As a reference, I've listed some insurance terms below, but insurance is not the only answer to risk management. We'll explore those too.

Peril: The insurance industry defines a "peril" as an event or circumstance that increases the potential for harm, loss, or damage. Perils can manifest in a myriad of forms, ranging from natural disasters to human-made incidents, and are the focal point of insurance coverage.

Damage: The aftermath of a perilous event leads to "damage," representing the tangible consequences incurred, be it financial or physical. This term encompasses the financial burden associated with restoring property or personal assets to their original state.

Premium: The "premium" is the monetary consideration the insured pays to the insurer in exchange for coverage. It serves as the economic foundation of the insurance contract, facilitating the transfer of risk.

Policy: The "policy" stands as the central document outlining the terms, conditions, and parameters of insurance coverage. It solidifies the contractual relationship between the insured and the insurer, delineating the extent of protection against specified perils.

Deductible: Integral to the insurance transaction, the "deductible" represents the initial amount the insured is responsible for shouldering before insurance coverage takes effect. It serves as a threshold that the insured must surpass before indemnification commences.

Coverage: The protection against damage is encapsulated by the term "coverage," signifying the extent of safeguarding against specific perils that an insurance policy bestows upon the insured. It constitutes the breadth of protection against potential losses.

Claim: The "claim" represents the formal request initiated by the insured, seeking compensation from the insurer who incurred the loss.

Liability: Of paramount importance in risk management, "liability" denotes legal responsibility arising from causing harm or damage to others or their property. Insurance often includes liability coverage to safeguard against legal and financial repercussions.

Insured: The person or thing to be protected by the coverage is the insured.

Indemnity: A concept at the core of insurance, "indemnity" assures the insured of financial restoration to their pre-loss state after a perilous event. It guarantees that the insured shall be made whole, and no better, following a covered loss. However, in life insurance, we cannot return the dead to a living state, so the indemnification is merely the cash pay-out agreed upon in the policy.

Loss: The tangible or intangible void left by a peril is the term "loss." It encompasses the financial or physical deficiency that arises from the occurrence of a covered event.

Replacement Cost: In the event of a loss, "replacement cost" coverage ensures that the insured can replace their damaged or lost property with a comparable asset of equivalent value. It facilitates the restoration of the insured's assets to their pre-loss condition.

These are some, not nearly all, of the common terms associated with insurance. Again, buying insurance is not always the right answer or even a possible answer. There is a subtle yet powerful strategy when dealing with risk. A financial martial art called avoidance. Let me side-step a moment and explain some non-financial risks and the obvious but unseen ways to implement avoidance.

A curious and painful phenomenon has emerged in the ever-expanding realm of vlogging, where digital storytellers document their passions and hobbies.

We know over a dozen people who vlog, and they all tell a story similar to this. Picture an enthusiastic vlogger utilizing the infamous selfie stick to record themselves in the midst of their adventures, only to be met with an unforeseen and abrupt collision between their phones and their unsuspecting faces. Ouch!

The issue is the attachment at the end of the selfie stick, entrusted with holding the phone securely, decides to call it quits. Suddenly, the phone makes a daring escape from its mount and sets itself on a collision course with the vlogger's nose, using the stick's body as a guide rail straight into their face.

What's the perilous possibility lurking here? It's the dreaded mount failure, culminating in a rather unpleasant facial smack. Solution – avoidance: simply abandoning the mount altogether and gripping the phone firmly by hand. By discarding the mount, they eliminate the risk of its betrayal.

Are there financial situations like the rebellious mount? Simple ones like, preventing the peril of overspending on Amazon.com by avoiding the online store altogether. Budgets are nicer, but if the problem is a deeper self-control issue, just avoid the temptation to impulse buy.

Other avoidance solutions may be less obvious.

When the temptation is also filled with good potential, we must evaluate the good result with the probability of success and then the pain of failure.

Expected Risk

Sarah Brielman had just turned 27, and her life seemed like a dream come true. As an HR professional working in Chicago, she had recently landed a job with a substantial salary, far beyond what she had ever imagined for herself at this stage in her career. Her friends and family were proud of her, and her achievements were celebrated, but Sarah slowly grew annoyed with her chosen career. "There were constant problems to solve, relationships to fix, and sugary ways to give bad news," Sarah explained to us.

After a year, she wanted out. Despite her success, Sarah yearned for something that didn't involve building other people's relationships. Instead, Sarah wanted to do woodworking, a hobby her father had and something they had done together for years. Rolltops, front falls, and davenports are tricky designs. She loved the feeling of fitting them together seamlessly, a reflection of her meticulous efforts. Every time she thought about woodworking, a feeling of joy and simplicity washed over her. No cranky personnel files to wade through, just the wood and her tools.

The thought of starting her own woodworking business lingered at the back of her mind. Practicality and fear of financial instability held her back. This woodworking venture would be risky, and she couldn't help but feel that abandoning her high-paying corporate job was foolish. Why risk financial security for a dream that could take years to materialize, if at all?

The allure ebbed and flowed for a bit until one day, after spending an entire weekend working on a small wooden side table in her garage, Sarah had an epiphany. She didn't have to quit to start. Sarah decided on a plan that combined her passion for woodworking with her need for financial stability. She would start her business small, creating one new piece of custom woodwork each month, all while continuing to work in HR. This way, she could slowly build momentum, test the market, and gauge whether her woodworking venture could become a viable source of income.

As Sarah began to share her work on social media, her creations quickly caught the eye of local enthusiasts. People admired the passion and attention to detail evident in her work. The response was overwhelming, and Sarah started to receive inquiries about purchasing her pieces.

With each successful sale, Sarah felt more empowered. The financial rewards were not as significant as her corporate job, but her satisfaction and fulfillment from each sale far surpassed any monetary gains. Her clients cherished her creations, and word-of-mouth started to spread.

Sarah's wooden masterpieces began to find homes in local cafes, boutique stores, and even some corporate offices. The positive feedback fueled her determination to grow her business further. Yet, she was mindful of not biting off more than she could chew. Sarah stayed true to her resolution of creating one piece a month, ensuring she didn't jeopardize her primary source of income.

As the months passed, Sarah's woodworking business continued to gain traction. She started receiving requests for custom designs and took immense pride in fulfilling each client's unique vision. Despite the financial challenges, Sarah discovered that risk management wasn't about avoiding her passion but about embracing it responsibly.

Her woodwork was not just functional furniture, but an extension of her soul poured into every curve and joint. This authenticity resonated with her customers, who appreciated the heart and soul infused into each creation. Sarah's reputation as a talented woodworker grew, and demand for her pieces increased steadily.

Eventually, Sarah found herself at a crossroads: her woodworking business was flourishing, and she had to decide whether to A. continue playing it safe in her corporate job or B. take a leap of faith and pursue her passion full-time."

Sarah chose to bring her passion to life. She took a calculated risk – not a foolish chance. She tendered her resignation and embraced the uncertainty of the entrepreneurial journey. The transition was undoubtedly scary, and there were moments of doubt, but Sarah's perseverance and belief in her craft carried her through.

As her business grew, so did her sense of fulfillment and achievement. Sarah realized that avoiding risk wasn't about staying stagnant but rather about managing it strategically. By starting small, she had allowed her passion to blossom while maintaining financial stability. The risk she had feared had transformed into the reward of living a life true to her dreams. She overcame a hurdle. Life was good and content, but it lacked the energy of achievement.

Years later, Sarah's custom woodwork business had become a resounding success. Her furniture pieces are cherished by customers across the country, and she has found her true happy place, where creativity and fulfillment flourish. The connection to her customers brings her a joy that the corporate world did not.

Sarah's story taught her that life was about taking calculated risks, using money as a smart tool, and embracing change and struggle. Avoiding risk wasn't cowardice; it was an intelligent strategy to safeguard her dreams until the time was right. The contentment and safety net of corporate HR work was getting in her way.

Sarah's tale serves as a guide, illuminating the path of risk endurance. The capacity of an individual to persist and withstand uncertainty, challenges, and potential losses while pursuing their goals is risk endurance. The management of risk has four moves to increase our tolerance and endurance: Avoidance, Mitigation, Transference, and Acceptance. Each move holds its unique charm and challenges, but by using money as our tool, we can confidently glide through the steps of this financial dance.

Move 1: Avoidance - Stepping Away from the Edge

In the art of risk management, sometimes the best step is not to step at all. Avoidance is the elegant maneuver of sidestepping hazards and potential pitfalls. Take the story of Sarah, a young professional with dreams of entrepreneurship. She dreams of quitting her corporate job to start her own business. However, she's burdened with student loan debt that might put her financial stability at risk. Sarah decides to delay her entrepreneurial venture until she has paid off a significant portion of her debt. By avoiding unnecessary financial strain, she sets herself up for future success.

Money as a Tool: In this scenario, Sarah uses money as a tool to strengthen her financial position. She allocates a portion of her income to aggressively pay down her student loans, reducing her debt-to-income ratio and improving her credit score. This prudent financial move gives her the freedom to venture into entrepreneurship with more confidence when the timing is right.

Move 2: Mitigation - Navigating the Rapids

As we walk through life, we'll encounter risks we can't completely avoid. That's where mitigation steps in - the art of lessening the impact of a potential risk. Consider Michael, a family man with a passion for travel. He enjoys exploring the world with his loved ones but worries about unforeseen health emergencies. Michael purchases comprehensive travel insurance that covers medical emergencies abroad. This way, if a health crisis arises during their adventures, his family can focus on healing rather than financial stress.

Money as a Tool: Michael uses money as a safety net to mitigate the financial impact of medical emergencies while traveling. By paying a reasonable insurance premium, he shifts the burden of potential medical expenses to the insurance company. This decision provides him with peace of mind during his journeys.

Move 3: Transference - Sharing the Load

In this intricate dance, sometimes, we seek assistance to navigate the complexities of risk. Transference is the act of sharing the burden with another party. Meet John, a diligent homeowner who recognizes the importance of safeguarding his property against unexpected disasters. John purchases homeowners' insurance, which covers damages from fire, theft, and natural disasters. By doing so, he transfers the financial responsibility of potential property damage to the insurance provider.

Money as a Tool: Through his homeowners' insurance, John strategically uses money to shift the financial burden of property damage to the insurance company. This frees him from the worry of substantial financial losses and enables him to focus on maintaining and cherishing his home.

Move 4: Acceptance - Embracing the Risk

As we twirl through life, some risks are part and parcel of our journey. Acceptance is the graceful bow to those unavoidable risks, acknowledging their presence while not allowing them to overshadow our financial aspirations.

Take Linda, an aspiring artist who is passionate about her craft. She chooses to pursue a career in a competitive and unpredictable industry, well aware of the inherent financial uncertainty. While acknowledging the financial risks, Linda embraces her dream, recognizing that creative fulfillment is worth the unpredictability.

Money as a Tool: Linda's acceptance of the inherent risk in her chosen career allows her to focus on honing her skills and building her artistic portfolio. She uses money as a means to budget wisely, saving for leaner times while investing in workshops and art supplies to enhance her craft further.

Marriage and Money

We've been talking a lot about your relationship with money. We have covered self-control when it comes to spending and saving and self-discipline as it relates to keeping track of the various money parts of your financial profile. These two keys unlocked the door to happiness, which we defined as the trifecta of a sense of achievement, contentment, and connection. Knowing this, we showed how money can be used as an additional tool to increase happiness.

But what happens when we must share money? Is there another component to your relationship with money when it comes to sharing the tool? Having a spouse to share life with means you also must share money. Much like you share a house, food, and rearing duties, money is a tool for both of you to sustain or reacquire the fleeting state of happiness.

The management of money in a marriage is often one-sided. This one-sided management leads to a relationship with two roles: 1. The authoritarian, and 2. The follower. Inherent tensions build in this type of relationship, because on the outside the relationship is supposed to be of equals, but it is seldom equal in practice. This doesn't mean spouses need to talk about every dollar spent, but if that don't talk at all financial tension grows. That tension can eventually snap the marriage in half, ending in divorce. Without co-management of finances, financial infidelity threatens the relationship. About 40% of divorce is due to a lack of open financial communication. Most commonly, we see this pattern:

It begins innocently with a bit of embarrassment or shame someone feels for themself or their actions. When it reaches a certain point, that shame turns to defensiveness, leading then to fear of conflict or argument arising. Hiding or lying about money begins. Soon it becomes elevated, and eventually, financial infidelity is routine.

Co-management doesn't mean each person is involved in every decision. It means that each person is aware of the general current situation and understands where they are headed. This includes the couple, together, have explored the risks and sacrifices determined. Each person's needs are being met, and roles of equal importance have been established, as well as the parameters of freedom.

Our clients have shown a consistent pattern of how happy and successful couples live financially together. We broke this down to a set of rules called "The Four Rules of Financial Marriage".

They are:
1. Teamwork (Communication and Awareness)
2. OPA! (Organize, Prioritize, Achieve)
3. Read-backs & Check-ins (K.I.S.S.)
4. Trust (Taming the Ego)

If this seems obvious, good. What makes this hard to follow is the implementation. Teamwork is the sum of communication with and awareness of the needs of your spouse. OPA! Is the path to action, first by organizing your financial life and then by prioritizing it.

Once those are completed, we simply need to get after it and achieve. Read-backs and check-ins are two ways to keep your plans simple. Simple plans allow the intended result to be clearly transferred into the minds of spouses and allow for deviations on paths set once real-life votes to disrupt you. When we allow for minor course corrections we show the fourth rule, trust. Trust is knowing that we don't always know what will happen, and if the intent of the joint goal is understood, then the correct will be effective enough. It may not be the best way, or the "right" way or certainly not our way, but we trust the other person to correct as needed because the end result is the goal, not the following of a particular path.

RULE 1 of Financial Marriage

Teamwork starts with communication. This is often a punchline that people gloss over. This happens because of a lack of understanding of what marriage communication means. It is the ability to feel safe saying, "I don't understand this." Moreover, the person you say it to must feel comfortable saying, "Me neither!" Instead of getting upset at the other delinquency of understanding, each spouse feels ownership in getting an answer they both understand.

The other component of teamwork is awareness. Awareness is the ability to anticipate the needs of the other person – being aware. If your wife likes milk in her tea at night, but you finished the milk this morning with your coffee, do you have the awareness while driving home from work to get more milk? Or, if know the milk has soured, do you pick up more? Do you call first to say, "Hey I noticed the milk was almost past due – should I get more?" This scenario happens a lot in the personal financial world with regards to HELOCs and credit. HELOCs, home equity lines of credit, are ways to take a loan out on a portion of your home. You get some cash to spend on a home improvement like a new driveway or roof and make monthly payments. Very similar to a credit card, but much lower interest rates.

The credit is usually near the price of the renovation or repair but not exact. Couples find themselves with excess cash and instead of making an extra repayment they increase lifestyle for a bit. When the amount is used up, they are suddenly out of milk (money). Anticipating the needs or expectations of your teammate, your spouse, can prevent tension. If you know the milk is souring, or the excess cash is dwindling, do let it be a surprise. Anticipate the others needs for: 1. Achievement, 2. Contentment, and 3. Connection.

Little Pockets; Big Impacts

Anne and Silvio epitomized teamwork in marriage. Anne, a dedicated teacher, and Silvio, a skilled handyman, supported each other through their respective professions and their shared dreams. If Anne needed a visual aid made for her classroom, Silvio could make it. When Silvio needed help understanding the family finances, Anne taught it to him.

Silvio had a business-oriented mind but not much patience for money matters. His superpower was finding hidden opportunities for real estate investing. Ultimately, this talent led him to consider real estate a full-time job. He shared this vision with Anne. Her enthusiasm matched his as she admired his determination.

Silvio took the first step, purchasing a weathered two-family duplex needing extensive renovation. Working together, they gathered every resource they had to transform the duplex into an inviting space for tenants. The cash flow was tight, even scary at times. Anne managed the finances, explaining the complexities to Silvio with her characteristic teaching skills. It was important they both understood the balancing act they were playing.

Anne began setting aside spare money, $50 here and $200 there, calling it her "little pocket." She explained to us, "I might have $60 left over for the week. If the kids were getting fed, and Silvio got his steak dinner on Sunday, I would put that money in a savings account. That was my little pocket. When Silvio needs money for a new property or repair, I can show him what's in my little pocket to help him."

Their marriage, marked by shared service and teamwork, flourished over more than 60 years. Their money, like Silvio's hammer, was a tool to live happily together.

RULE 2 of Financial Marriage

The second rule of financial marriage is what we call OPA! Organize, prioritize, and achieve. This is important in marriage because life makes things messy, our priorities can change, and motivation to keep on-plan can diminish.

Staying organized keeps the picture of your finances in focus. The more moving parts we have, the harder it is to see the forest through the trees. If things are in focus, we will have an easier time pivoting as priorities shift. Change can be hard and cluttering up our finances with misaligned priorities can kill effort. Staying motivated is the only way to continue to make progress. Motivation is clarity of path and the chosen intensity with which we walk it. If we even ask, "Wait, why are we doing this," we know motivation to the goal is waning.

Share with your spouse the HOGG method and Motivation = Clarity + Intensity.

RULE 3 of Financial Marriage

Since action is key, how can we stay motivated? How do we get clarity and intensity? Clients unanimously echo the sentiment of the adage, "Keep it Simple Stupid." Our third rule of financial marriage is simple plans. Simple doesn't mean ineffective. In fact, quite the opposite. The more complex a plan is, the more moving parts there are, the more instances of potential failure there will be. The spirit of Simple Plans is "good enough" to communicate the intent of the goal and why the goal exists. If this can be achieved, adjustments can be made more easily when needed.

If the plan is to pay off mortgage debt faster, making a simple plan, like adding $1000/month to your payment, will be way more effective than trying to time extra payments based on fluctuations in the rates, evolving tax optimization strategies, the current M2 deposits in the federal banking system, stock market valuation trading, or even good deals on short terms loan tranches like new car loans. That all seems complex, right? Keeping track of all that would not be effective because we would be paralyze into inaction. Keeping the plan simple will add automaticity to the plan. "Keep moving forward" is a better adage than "maximize your financial decisions"

Rule 4 of Financial Marriage

Lastly, our fourth rule is trust. There's a problem with how people think of trust, some people believe trust is earned. TRUST IS NOT EARNED. Stop saying it! Trust is given and taken away. It is not earned. If someone proves to you that they can do something for you, you believe them. Belief is earned. Trust is given.

I believe parachutes work. I've seen it. When I am standing at the door of a plane about to jump out, I trust mine will work. I believe my daughter can make me a good cup of coffee. I trust the airport Starbucks to do the same. Belief is earned, trust is given. Maybe you believe in your Starbucks barista, terrific, but before you did, you trusted in them.

Trust has to do with growing belief in your teammate, your spouse; they are working for the benefit of the couple and not just themselves. We can't live happily if we need to micromanage each other. Further, we cannot live happily if we are constantly being micromanaged. If a mistake is made, recognize it and remedy it. Each spouse must be willing to say it was their mistake.

Keelie: You bought the wrong diapers.

Liam: But these were on sale.

Keelie: These don't have the wetness indicator.

Liam: Is that more important than saving money?

Keelie: Yes. I often must change him in the car, and it's very inconvenient.

Liam: Got it. My mistake. I should have asked before assuming all diapers were the same.

Keelie: No problem, I should have explained why I put that brand specifically on the shopping list.

Keelie asked Liam for help in shopping (Teamwork). She knew he would need a list for him to follow and make the purchases (OPA!). Keelie put a specific brand on the list to prevent confusion (Simple). Liam got the list but noticed a better deal on a different brand and made the choice to buy the less expensive brand. When he got home, Liam learned he got the wrong brand and found out why.

Both spouses took ownership of the error because they understood the error wasn't spiteful, and both could see how they could have prevented the mis-purchase. (Trust). They believe the other acted in good faith to accomplish something. When things went wrong, which they do, they learned from their mistake together.

Kids and Money

Let's continue our exploration of money and the relationship with others. Specifically, our kids. We want to equip you with some practical tools to explain and teach the next generation the purpose of money, how it works, and how to be financially fit. Depending on the age of the child, different methods and topics should be selected. We will cover examples for younger and older kids based on the following four topics.

Purpose of Money | Value Exchange: If money is a tool, there must be more than one tool for different financial jobs and task. We will explore the concepts of favor, barter, payment, and credit, revealing their intricate roles in the world of finance.

Forms of Money: The philosophical purpose needs a form. Let's reaffirm our understanding the tangible and intangible forms of currency—ranging from cash and coins to checks and credit cards—this section unveils the multifaceted nature of money itself.

Income Types: Money flows into our lives in different ways. A dollar of salary is worth less to us in the end than a dollar of capital gains. The intricacies of active, passive, and portfolio income streams are dissected in this portion, offering a nuanced perspective on the avenues through which money flows.

Financial Fitness | Good Habits: A favorite analogy of mine is physical fitness and financial fitness. If you don't make millions, are you financially unfit? If you can't bench press 200lbs, are you financially unfit? Of course not, to both. In this section we will uncover some good money habits, underscoring their role in shaping a fiscally fit future.

Section 1: Purpose of Money | Value Exchange

Money is convenient. It's hard to know how many chickens I need to trade or exchange for a haircut. How many favors do I owe for a car wash? Money and credit make the transacting or transfer of value easier, whether for a good or a service. Financial terms such as favor, barter, payment, and credit are integral components of economic value transactions, each with distinct characteristics and implications.

A favor in a financial context often refers to an act of kindness or assistance extended to someone without a specified quid pro quo. It generally lacks a direct exchange of goods, services, or money. Favors may have social or personal significance, but they typically don't carry the structured and measurable attributes of financial transactions. They rely heavily on interpersonal relationships and can't be quantified or standardized like other financial terms.

Barter is a historical method of exchange in which goods and services are directly swapped for other goods and services without using money as an intermediary. In a barter transaction, each party must possess something the other desires, creating a double coincidence of wants. The challenge with barter lies in finding suitable trading partners and reaching agreements on the relative value of items being exchanged. Barter systems lack the efficiency and flexibility of modern monetary systems, as they can be cumbersome, impractical, and hindered by indivisibility or perishability of goods.

Payment is the transfer of value in the form of money to fulfill an obligation for goods, services, or debts. It is a fundamental aspect of financial transactions in modern economies. Payments can be made using various mediums, including cash, checks, electronic funds transfers, credit cards, and digital wallets. Payments represent the final step of a transaction, where the recipient receives compensation for goods or services provided. The timeliness and security of payments are critical to maintaining trust between parties and sustaining economic activity.

Credit: Credit refers to the arrangement in which one party lends money, goods, or services to another party with the expectation of being repaid in the future. It involves trust that the borrower will honor the debt according to agreed terms. Credit plays a pivotal role in modern economies, facilitating consumption, investment, and economic growth. Credit can take various forms, such as bank loans, mortgages, credit cards, and trade credit. It allows individuals and businesses to access resources they might not immediately possess, enabling them to make purchases or investments and pay back over time.

For Younger Children

Game 1: The Happiness Path

Objective: This game introduces the concept of favors, how they make someone feel to get a favor, and how it feels to plan and give a favor to someone else. Favors are little bits of happiness, so we will use achievement, contentment, and connection as our guides to the happiness path.

How to Play:

1. Number of Players: This game can be played with one child or a group of kids.

2. Understanding Favors: Begin by explaining the concept of favors - doing something nice for someone without expecting payment or reciprocity (a return favor) but for the purpose of making something better, like achievement, contentment, connection.

3. Selecting Recipients: Each player should think of two people. Examples: a family member, a friend, a neighbor.

4. Planning Favors: For each of person chosen, the player should think of three nice things to do for them. One for increasing happiness because of achievement, one for contentment, and one for connection. For example, a big sister might want to do something for her little sister.

Achievement: Painting workshop: complete a painting about favorite animal. Remember achievement is about striving or overcoming an obstacle. The blank piece of paper turns into art. Little sister can try to paint it again and again until she is happy with the result.

Contentment: Big sister clears little sister's plate at the dinner table. A simple quick gesture that should elicit a "Thank you" showing gratitude which is a form of contentment.

Connection: Big sister reads bedtime story to little sister. They are sharing in the story and sharing the experience together.

- Write down the planned favors and leave space to mark them as completed. Draw a big box next to each favor idea.

- Did you paint with little sister? Check!

- Did you clear her spot at the dinner table? Check!

- Did you read to her at bedtime? Check!

This nice thing about this step of the game is making a plan, keeping it simple, and tracking actions taken.

5. Completing Favors:
- Give some timeline to complete the happiness favors, like 24 hours.

6. Discussion:
After the favors are completed, gather the players to discuss how favors can create a sense of mutual happiness between the favor giver and the favor receiver. Did their favors work?

Note:
- Emphasize the importance of the act of giving, and how it can positively impact both the giver and the recipient. Explore the ideas of happiness in terms of did they produce achievement for the person, contentment, or connection.

Game 2: Barter Bucks
Objective: This game is designed for younger children aged 7-13 to teach them about the concepts of barter, effort, and the value of money. The goal is to help them understand that their efforts lead to cap-

ital and the importance of choosing the most cost-effective means of obtaining what they desire.

How to Play:

1. Setting Objectives:

- Ask the child to pick three things they would like to acquire, such as a new toy, movie tickets, or dinner at their favorite restaurant.

2. Earning Currency:

- Explain that they can obtain these items using two different types of currency:

- Barter Bucks: A special currency earned by completing chores.

- Real Money: The standard currency used for everyday purchases.

3. Chore Equivalents:

- Inform the child that each chore they complete is worth either one real dollar or three Barter Bucks.

- They have the flexibility to choose which currency they wish to earn for each chore.

4. Accumulating Currency:

- Over the course of a month, the child will accumulate both Barter Bucks and real money as they continue to complete chores.

5. Comparison and Decision:

- Encourage the child to compare their accumulated Barter Bucks and real money.

- Help them understand the value of both currencies and how they were earned.

6. Spending Choices:

- At the end of the month, the child will have noticed that they may have more Barter Bucks than real money.

- Explain that they have the choice to spend their Barter Bucks or real money for the items they desire.

7. Conversion Test:

- To spend Barter Bucks, the child must convert them to real dollars. This involves a simple math test where they calculate the equivalent value of their Barter Bucks in real dollars.

Lessons:

- **Lesson 1:** Through this game, the child will realize that bartering can be more cost-effective based on their effort.

- **Lesson 2:** Over time, as they spend little to no real dollars, they will have accumulated real dollars, which are more convenient for transactions. This demonstrates the importance of choosing the most convenient tool to reach their financial goals.

Note:

- This game aims to teach valuable life lessons about the relationship between effort, different types of capital, and the convenience of various forms of currency.

For Older Children

Teaching financial concepts like "cash money" and "credit" to older kids can be both educational and engaging. Try Monopoly with a Twist is a unique variation of the classic board game, tailored for teenagers seeking an exciting and educational gaming experience. In this version, we introduce a few intriguing twists to teach players about money management, property ownership, and the concept of leveraging credit.

The game is limited to a maximum of six circuits around the board, concluding when the first player successfully completes their sixth round. What sets this version apart is that players have the option to use unlimited credit for property acquisitions until they land in jail. It's a test of financial strategy where players must track their credit usage and decide when to settle their debts.

When players pass GO, they are faced with a critical decision – either pay off their entire outstanding credit plus a 10% fee, or opt for a 20% payment of their total debt. This choice can make or break their financial empire. The game's ultimate objective is to explore whether using credit to build a real estate empire was a savvy choice and how much luck played a role in the journey. The victor is determined by calculating the total property values and subtracting the outstanding debts. Keep in mind that even when behind bars, players can still rake in rent.

It might look like this:

Certainly! Here's a timeline of some possible outcomes for a game of Monopoly with a Twist, played by four players:

Round 1:

1. Players start with initial funds and begin their first circuit around the board.

2. Players use unlimited credit to acquire properties strategically.

3. Some players choose to accumulate more debt to invest in high-value properties, while others play it safe.

4. Players land on Chance and Community Chest cards, which may affect their finances positively or negatively.

5. The first player successfully completes their first round, and the game continues.

Round 2:

6. Players continue to make decisions about when to settle their debts and whether to pay off their credit when passing GO.

7. Some players may start feeling the pressure of accumulating debt and make their first debt settlement.

8. Property values vary as players upgrade their properties.

9. Players may start trading properties and making deals to strengthen their positions.

10. The second player completes their first circuit around the board.

Round 3:

11. Debt management becomes crucial as players have more properties and debts.

12. Some players may struggle to pay off their debts on each pass of GO.

13. Players continue to invest in properties and develop their real estate empires.

14. The third player completes their first circuit around the board.

Round 4:

15. Debt becomes a significant factor for most players as they enter the middle phase of the game.

16. Property values increase as players improve their properties.

17. Some players may be forced to mortgage properties to settle their debts.

18. The fourth player completes their first circuit around the board.

Round 5:

19. Players continue to make strategic decisions about when to settle debts and when to accumulate more properties.

20. Some players may have a substantial real estate empire, while others may be struggling with debts.

21. The first player successfully completes their fifth round, and the game is nearing its end.

Round 6:

22. Players make their final decisions regarding debt and property management.

23. The tension increases as players calculate their total property values and outstanding debts.

24. The second player successfully completes their fifth round.

25. The game concludes when the first player successfully completes their sixth round.

End of Game:

26. All players calculate their total property values and subtract their outstanding debts.

27. The victor is determined by the player with the highest net worth after settling debts.

28. The game highlights the role of strategy and luck in building a financial empire.

Each game will have its twists and turns, with players making different choices along the way. The outcome will depend on their strategic thinking, property acquisitions, and debt management skills.

Section 2: Forms of Money

Cash, checks, and credit cards stand as the three dominant methods of financial transactions, each with unique attributes and utility. Understanding the when, where, and how to deploy these monetary forms is both an exercise in knowledge and a potential catalyst for reshaping our financial habits and attitudes, influencing our relationship with money itself.

Cash, the physical manifestation of a nation's currency, holds the longstanding moniker "Cash is King." For decades, it has been seen as the favorite form of money since it is backed by the full faith and credit of the government's ability to levy taxes. Cash includes coins and banknotes bearing the imprints of authority and legitimacy. Its most undeniable quality is tangibility. This quality makes cash particularly suitable for small-scale, face-to-face transactions.

Another highly desirable quality of cash is the privacy it offers. Cash transactions, devoid of digital footprints or paper trails, facilitate a level of anonymity that contrasts sharply with their electronic counterparts or notes of promise like checks.

Checks, an old instrument of financial promise, occupy a distinct space in the methods of payment. A check is a written directive from an account holder to a bank, instructing the transfer of a specified amount to the payee (the person or legal entity receiving the funds). Checks retain a semblance of the traditional, blending the art of penmanship with society's honesty. Both penmanship and honesty have slipped in the modern world, but checks are still widely used.

One of the noteworthy features of checks lies in their issuer. Unlike cash, which emanates from the central authority, the government, checks are a product of individuals or businesses. A check serves as an embodiment of trust – a commitment to honor the written promise with available funds. This commitment is not instantaneous, however. Clearing a check involves several steps, often several days before the funds become accessible to the recipient. Mobile banking has helped consumers by freeing them from the burden of driving to the bank to make deposits. Further, checks leave an indelible paper trail. This quality aids in record-keeping and financial management, showing a path through the labyrinth of transactions.

Leverage is wonderful until you fall off the ledge. Credit cards have emerged as quintessential conduits of consumer empowerment. These plastic gateways to credit offer a symbiotic relationship between financial institutions and consumers, facilitating seamless transactions on a global scale. Unlike cash and checks, which involve existing funds, credit cards extend a line of credit, allowing users to borrow up to a predetermined limit. This credit can be employed for purchases, effectively bridging temporal gaps between desire and financial liquidity.

The cornerstone of credit card utility is its convenience. They are a universal currency, transcending borders and currencies. The versatility they offer extends from brick-and-mortar stores to the vast expanse of the online marketplace. This convenience, however, bears a caveat: the responsibility of repayment.

Many credit cards offer rewards programs, cash-back incentives, and exclusive access to events and experiences, tethering personal spending habits to benefits. Yet, the allure of rewards can become a double-edged sword, potentially encouraging impulsive spending if not manage judiciously.

A huge benefit of credit cards is the security blanket credit cards provide. Cyber threats, fraud, and identity threats can be minimized by the shield credit cards offer against unauthorized transactions. Consumers can contest and reverse charges in case of discrepancies, fostering a sense of safety absent in cash or checks.

For Young Children

Let's concentrate on cash with the younger kids first. As a basic practice, we want to rethink the "piggy bank." Instead of using a fancy piggy bank, you can go for a clear plastic jug. The idea is to make money less mysterious and help them get used to it. We want money to be seen as a useful thing, not something to idolize. Instead of keeping it locked up, let them have access to it. They can explore and play around with it. Using a clear bottle will also let them watch as their money grows over time.

Cash Play: Get some coins and bills – have a variety

Version 1. Have your child organize them into piles of similar value.

Version 2. Mix up all the coins and bills. Then, time them and see how long it takes to organize the bills and coins.

Version 3. Organize the bills and coins again, but put them in piles based on value, e.g. Pennies go all the way to the left, and $5 bills go all the way to the right. Put the remaining in between based on ascending value, right to left. (This is like a cash register.)

Version 4. How to make change. Set prices for various items in your house and have your child purchase them. Don't give them all the coins and bills, only the larger denominations. You act as the cashier and have to make change for them. Then switch roles once they get the game and have them make change.

For Older Children

Prepare a discussion about when to use cash, credit, or check. Think of 50 things and talk about when you would use each form and why. Sometimes there is more than one "best way" because of particular circumstances. Great! Explain the reasoning.

Then ask them when and why they would use each form to purchase things on the list.

Stumped as to what to put on the list? Understandable. People spend money on a wide variety of items and expenses in their daily lives. Expenditures often start with the essentials like housing costs, utilities, groceries, and transportation, including car payments and gas. Health-related expenses, such as healthcare and insurance, are common, as are educational costs, including tuition and textbooks. People also allocate a portion of their budget to clothing, dining out, and various forms of entertainment, such as movies and concerts. Technology and communication needs are met through cell phone and internet bills, while personal care products like shampoo and soap are recurring expenses. Maintaining the home is essential, so funds are allocated for repairs and maintenance. Many also invest in gym memberships to stay fit.

Travel and leisure pursuits, such as flights and hotel stays, contribute to a significant part of expenditures, while safeguarding assets involves paying for insurance, including car, life, and home insurance. People save and invest for their future, making contributions to retirement accounts and handling their taxes, including income and property taxes. Families with children spend on childcare and day-care, and pet owners allocate funds for pet expenses, such as food and veterinary visits. Special occasions and holidays often necessitate purchasing gifts and staying connected in the digital age involves expenses related to electronics, including computers and smartphones.

Hobbies and interests vary, leading to purchases of sports equipment, art supplies, and other supplies related to personal interests. Furniture and home decor contribute to creating a comfortable living space. Subscription services, such as Netflix and Spotify, are popular, as are occasional indulgences in alcoholic beverages and dining out. Convenience plays a role in spending on fast food and beverages like coffee. Home appliances, like refrigerators and washing machines, are vital household items, and avid readers invest in books and magazines. Cable or satellite TV subscriptions and home security systems are common, as are purchases related to outdoor activities, such as bicycles and camping gear.

Personal grooming, like haircuts and makeup, is a routine expense, and vehicles require car insurance and regular maintenance. Public transportation passes help with commuting in urban areas. Protecting one's home is a priority, resulting in home insurance expenses. Many people generously contribute to charities through donations, and their spending extends to jewelry, vehicles, and their maintenance. Students often have loans to repay, and electronics accessories, like phone cases and chargers, are everyday necessities. Property taxes contribute to local infrastructure and services, while tickets to sporting events and subscriptions to magazines keep people entertained.

Additional services like home cleaning, art classes, and rental fees for equipment or venues come into play. Professional services in areas such as law and accounting have associated fees, as do pet care services like grooming and boarding. Antiques and collectibles appeal to enthusiasts who allocate a budget for such acquisitions. Student loans can be a significant financial burden, and electronic accessories and property taxes continue to factor into expenses. Attending sporting events and subscribing to magazines offer entertainment options, and home cleaning services help maintain a tidy living space. Art classes and workshops, along with rental fees for equipment or venues, may be part of individual interests.

Financial advisors provide expertise for a fee, and online courses offer valuable learning opportunities. Photography equipment is an investment for photography enthusiasts, while spa and wellness treatments provide relaxation and self-care. Vintage items and video games appeal to a diverse range of interests, and home renovation projects allow homeowners to enhance their living spaces. Music lessons are common expenses, as are extracurricular activities for children. Investment management services and aquarium or terrarium supplies cater to specific needs. Supplies for kids' art activities and professional photography services contribute to expenditures. Repair services for plumbing and electrical issues are essential, as are season tickets to sports events and board games and puzzles for family entertainment.

Collectible toys and art supplies for adults are part of various hobbies, and business coaching or mentoring services assist entrepreneurs. Tickets to theater performances offer cultural experiences, while hobby-related travel takes enthusiasts to exciting destinations. Art gallery visits may be a form of entertainment, and membership fees for clubs or associations allow individuals to participate in various communities. Collectibles like trading cards and rare coins or currency appeal to collectors. Motorcycling gear is an investment for enthusiasts, and wine and wine-related products cater to connoisseurs. Archery equipment rounds out the diverse list of items and expenses people spend their money on.

Section 3: Income Types | Active, Passive, and Portfolio

Active Income is the money you earn through your direct efforts and work. When you have a job, and you're actively doing tasks or providing services, you receive active income. It includes the wages you get paid for your work, commissions if you sell things, and the money you make if you run your own business. This type of income is like the traditional way of earning money by putting in your time and skills.

Passive income is a bit different. It's the money that comes to you without needing constant active involvement. This type of income is generated from initial investments or activities that you set up, and then they continue to make money with less ongoing work. For example, if you own a rental property, you'll receive rent regularly without having to do daily work for it. Similarly, if you invest in stocks or bonds, you can earn money through dividends and capital appreciation without actively managing them all the time.

Lastly, we have portfolio income, which is tied to your investments. When you put your money into things like stocks, bonds, or real estate, the money you make from the increase in their value is considered portfolio income. If the value of your investments goes up and you sell them for a higher price, that's capital gains – a type of portfolio income. Additionally, if you receive regular payments from your investments, like interest from bonds or dividends from stocks, that also falls under portfolio income. It's a way of making money from the growth and earnings of your investment portfolio.

For Both Young Children and Older Children

I don't want you to think we suggest you must give your kids an allowance. That's completely up to you. Further, I don't want you to go broke during this, so please feel free to adjust as needed. We want to impart to the kids that income, whatever its form, is an incentive. Active and passive income both have effort involved. Active income is cause and effect, passive income is setting up a system to get income without dedicated effort.

With that said, let's talk about the task of kids cleaning their bedrooms. There are two components: Cleaning and Keeping it Clean. If your kid cleans their room, they have spent a specific amount of time on the act of cleaning up the whole room, which could include old dishes to the sink, two loads of laundry, organized desk, putting away art supplies, vacuuming/sweeping, etc. For this effort, let's say you pay them $5. Every Saturday night, they will "clean their room" and get $5. This is active income. If, however, they keep their room clean, i.e., they have developed a habit and system to put their clothes in the hamper each day, not bring food into their room, art supplies get put away right after use, then they have passively earned an allowance each day. On Saturday night, they get rewarded with $1 for every day that week they kept their room clean – earning them a potential income of $7.

Adding in the concept of a portfolio, which is an investment of some kind, have them agree to buy into their younger sibling's success. They will purchase $0.30 a day ($2.10/week) of their younger brother's success. If little Joey keeps his room clean all week, big brother will get an extra $0.50/day or $3.50 on Saturday night. Let's say Joey does keep his room clean. What would that look like?

Big brother:

Week 1

$7 - $2.10 (Joey Stock) = $4.90 Cash after Week 1

Week 2

$7+$3.50 - $2.10 = $8.40 Cash after Week 2

If Joey doesn't do it, instead of big brother getting $7/ week, he only gets $4.90. That's less than just cleaning his room once a week! So, the question becomes:

Is Little Joey a good investment?

Section 4: Financial Fitness | Good Habits

Habits make doing the right thing easier. Once something is a habit, the burden of it lessens. If we teach our kids not just skills but the habits to use the skill, hopefully, they will not grow up to be in the 75% of Americans who suffer from monthly financial anxiety. Habits are the way to financial security. Have you ever tried to teach your kids to bring their dinner dishes to the sink? Or load the dishwasher? It is perplexingly hard to get them to do it the first several times. But after a while, you notice them getting up from the table, plate and cup in hand, and making the trek into the kitchen. This is the pilgrimage of cleanliness in our house. It's wonderful. What habits about money can I teach them, like clearing their place at the table?

Saving Money:

• Piggy Bank or Jar: Younger kids can start with a piggy bank or a clear jar to visibly see their savings grow. Whenever they receive money, encourage them to put a portion of it into their savings container.

• Savings Account: As they get older, consider opening a savings account for your child. Take them to the bank to make deposits and help them keep track of their account balance.

• Goal Setting: Help your child set savings goals, such as saving for a toy, a special outing, or even a larger purchase. This provides motivation and a sense of accomplishment when they reach their goals.

Delayed Gratification:

• Wish List: When your child expresses a desire for a new toy or item, have them add it to a wish list. Encourage them to wait a certain period before making a purchase, allowing time to consider if they really want or need it.

• Earning through Chores: Linking chores to earning money can teach kids that they need to work and save up before they can buy something they want.

• Reward Systems: Implement a reward system

where delayed gratification is rewarded. For example, if they wait a certain amount of time before spending, they might earn a small bonus.

Comparison Shopping:

• Store Visits: Take your child to the store and involve them in shopping decisions. Show them how to compare prices, read labels, and consider factors like quality and value.

• Online Shopping: If shopping online, sit down with your child and compare prices from different websites. Discuss the importance of looking for deals, free shipping, and customer reviews.

• Price Tracking: Encourage your child to track the prices of items they're interested in over time. This can help them understand fluctuations in prices and make informed decisions.

Tracking and Budgeting:

• Allowance Management: If your child receives an allowance, help them manage it. Have them allocate a portion to savings, spending, and giving. Provide a simple ledger or spreadsheet to track these categories.

• Envelope System: Using envelopes labeled with categories (e.g., saving, spending, giving), help your child allocate their money accordingly. This gives them a tangible way to manage their funds.

• Digital Tools: Introduce your child to age-appropriate budgeting apps or tools. These tools can help them track their income and expenses, set goals, and visualize their financial progress.

The pains and burdens of responsible actions are quelled by habits. We want them to think, "Yeah, this is just what we do – we save 20%, we buy it only when we have the many, we confirm our accounts and activities – that's just what we do." They don't have any bad habits with money yet. Help them get started down the right path that took us much longer to forge.

Connie and Glen Test

Our relationships with ourselves, our spouses, our children, our friends, and our co-workers will all be affected by money in some way or another. Using money as a tool by spending, borrowing, saving, or making makes it one of the most ubiquitous tools we will ever have. We have explored what money is, how money works, and when to use it. The most important exploration is why. Why is money so important? It allows us more freedom than any other tool because of its remarkably fungible nature.

It can also be a tool for disaster. If we don't respect or take care of this tool, it can't and won't take care of us. To know that most Americans are emotionally burdened with financial worry saddens me. Please help others by using the concepts in this book.

I'll leave you with this last story and see if you can piece out the foundations of happiness and misalignment – this is your test to help others.

Choose happiness.

The story of Connie and Glenn.

"We're getting a divorce." I watched Connie for a moment after she said it. Her hands were wrapped around her teacup. My pause suggested I was waiting for a punchline. What kind of ending does this joke have," I thought to myself. She spoke again, "But we want you to help us get through the money part of it."

Connie and Glenn had been clients for years. They have 5 adult children, all of whom I've watched go through college and start meaningful lives. Glenn retired from teaching high school mathematics about 10 years ago. Connie had led a huge division at an insurance company and retired 2 years ago at age 65. They built a house in Florida together and enjoyed being grandparents. They were living the American Dream.

Stunned and perplexed, I took a breath and repeated what I thought I heard. "You have both decided to divorce each other, and you want us to help you split the assets equally, is that right?"

"Yes," Glenn said.

These are awkward conversations, and I have learned to be careful about asking questions that are too personal. I know they are not getting divorced today, and if they wish to share the reasons, they can later.

"Okay, well, I can do that. May I propose I spend some time with the balance sheet and how to equitably split things? It should be simple. We can use the estate plan as a template. In the meantime, if either of you already have ideas about how things should be split, I can consider that input." They both agreed. I told them I'd call each individually to chat about ideas, and then together; we could all meet to discuss the preliminary splitting of assets.

The meeting lasted less than 10 minutes. A record. I shook their hands and asked them what their plans were for the afternoon. Excited to share, Connie said, "We're going to do some shopping for the grandkids and then get lunch in West Hartford." Glenn helped Connie with her coat, and they left. Together.

I reorganized their assets over the next few hours and created two balance sheets. I guessed who would want non-liquid assets like houses and cars and devised an equalizer formula that would counterbalance discrepancies if everyone remained logical. Projecting out over the next ten years, Glenn and Connie could reasonably expect what their financial life would be going forward. Together, they had no debt, with about $4 million saved in retirement accounts and personal investment accounts. Their combined spending was $250,000 per year. Financially, life was easy for them. Separately, it got a little tighter but still nice. They would need to spend about $185,000 per year to get a similar lifestyle. Not as easy, but still very doable.

Later that week, I spoke to both on the phone. First, Glenn. He told me this was Connie's idea, and though he was shocked, he was starting to process that this was really happening. "She hasn't been happy for a few months, maybe a year. Since we moved to Florida, she has had a tough time adjusting. At first, Connie was busy making our new home and putting the final touches on things. We made some friends and would do the rounds hosting and being hosted at each other's homes. This was really nice. She had been texting and Facebooking with friends at home, in Connecticut, a lot. It's been tough to get her out to see people - ya know in real time - in Florida. Something's off. I just don't know what."

Glenn went on to describe all the little house projects Connie did. Something always felt not-quite-done. Connie liked the new friends, but she didn't seek them out to do things. They politely included her in activities and gatherings. "They would come over the house, and I could hear Connie laughing and getting along well, but afterwards, she would tell me all about the friends and their houses and cars and careers. She'd always compare our situation to theirs. "They can't have more than us, how can they afford that sort of thing." I was starting to sense Connie wasn't unhappy with Glenn but with her life. When Glenn left, Connie called and asked for an appointment with us.

Two days later, Connie sat in our office, quietly reviewing the balance sheet split. I admired her keen financial sense. She knew numbers and could see how they related to each other. If we made a small adjustment on one line, she was able to mentally carry through to know the impact somewhere else. It was fun working with her.

"This is great!"

"Is there anything you'd change?"

"I'll sit with it for a while, but I like the structure. Very helpful. I like how you offset real estate with the IRA and cash. It can go either way — whoever gets the house…" Connie trailed off.

Suddenly, the numbers weren't numbers. The number became the house. She had spent hours making that house just the way she liked it. "I don't know, maybe I should keep the house. But then I'd have to give Glenn more of the IRA. That doesn't seem fair, that money I made." The plan started to unravel.

"And if you take the house, how much do you think is fair to give Glenn?"

"Ugh," Connie revved up, "maybe that's right, Glenn takes the house, and I keep more of the IRA." She followed the numbers through.

"Well, that doesn't leave much in the way of cash flow for Glenn. Are you okay if he sells the house, takes that money, and gets something smaller?"

"He can't sell it! I worked hard on that house. I built and furnished that house for him —

I'll give him more so he can afford it."

"Help me understand why is it important that Glenn stays in the house?"

"It just seems like a waste," Connie said harshly.

"What a waste?"

"A waste of money," She quipped quickly. "And time."

"Let's just blue-sky this: What if Glenn takes the house, doesn't need more money, and is fine? Where are you going to live? Are you going to buy another place nearby? Move to a different part of Florida?"

"No. I'll probably move back to Connecticut. Be closer to the grandkids. I still have lots of friends here. I miss them. The people in Florida are nice, but it's always an event to get together. I feel like I'm interviewing new friends — even being interviewed. There's probably a little bit of boredom in there too. After retiring and making the house just right, I feel like I don't have anything to do. That just makes me feel more anxious about missing the grandkids — time is ticking, and more and more, I'm not part of their lives. I hate it." She paused, teary.

Detached and resolved, she continued, "Ok, Glenn can sell the house if he needs to.

What's next?"

Connie had a sense of accomplishment and achievement for building the new home for her husband. But it came at a price that wasn't on the balance sheet. She removed herself from the place and situation, which made her happy. Routine social behavior had locked her into a path to retire, move to Florida, and build a nice "dream" home. When she realized her error, her ego wouldn't let her admit to others she had made a huge mistake and spent hundreds of thousands of dollars doing it. This is a real and common occurrence. When we let ourselves be defined by our things and money, our decisions become focused on the superficial. We act out of boredom and have a tough time taking proper corrective steps because of the fear of looking dumb.

To her credit, Connie saw her mistakes and bravely admitted them to Glenn. After some more calls and meetings with me and seeking a professional marriage counselor, they reconciled. The Florida home was sold, and they purchased a smaller house in Connecticut near the grandkids. Connie and Glenn could easily be viewed as a lesson of financial failure, but I see it as a story of growth and understanding that merely included some financial pain. They've never been happier than they are now.

www.ingramcontent.com/pod-product-compliance
Lightning Source LLC
Chambersburg PA
CBHW032122090426
42743CB00007B/425